TRUST ME, I'M HUMAN

Copyright © Mick Mooney, 2018
First Published 2018
Published by RedFox Books
email: media@mickmooney.com
URL: mickmooney.com

Trust Me, I'm Human
Mooney, Mick
ISBN: 9780648101444

REDFOX Books
Stories Worth Churning

For Mira, Liv & Luke.
You bring out the best in me.
Thank you.

Praise for Trust Me, I'm Human

I had the opportunity to read an advance copy of Trust Me, I'm Human and quite frankly I couldn't put it down! There are so many "aha" moments – the author managed to collate a million of my thoughts into one sentence.

The chapter on Values and Leadership comes at an opportune time because as a facilitator/coach I am currently training a group on leadership. I have devised an activity for them to do to see if their personal values align with the organisation's values and I was struggling with how to convey the importance of value alignment in leadership.

This book has me thinking of ways to portray information, especially new concepts, in a story form first before we get into the nitty-gritty. Thank you for stretching me!

- Cindy Donald

Trust me, I'm Human by Mick Mooney is filled with nuggets of gold. I found myself continually pausing to write down notes from what I was reading. As a millennial, I am excited to see this book being put in the hands of corporate leaders globally as I feel that the messages conveyed are critical to the evolution of business and ultimately society. From my experience in corporate, when effective storytelling and connection in the workplace has been prevalent, my level of inspiration and quality of output improves tenfold. This book isn't just a "here's why it's important" … it's a "here's how to action it" too. Very grateful to have read this book and I'm looking forward to witnessing and experiencing its impact in the business world moving forward.

- Kevin Adams

Trust Me, I'm Human will stimulate managers across all industries to reflect on the way that they interact with their employees, offering an alternative to traditional methods to improve employee engagement and connection in the workplace. The science behind using storytelling as an engagement tool is something I wasn't aware of before myself, yet telling meaningful stories to clearly get my point across is something that I do all the time. Every professional needs to read this book, especially those who rely solely on showing data, numbers and stats using traditional methods of presenting information to their employees.

Mick Mooney utilises his clear, simple language to communicate to us, the reader, about the how and why of storytelling as the sharpest tool in any manager's toolkit.

My favourite phrase in the book is, "Humans make lousy robots."

How true. We all need stimulation, connectivity with others, and most of all, to live our values, not just say them out loud.

- *Jennifer Maly*

This book was easy for me to read. It kept my attention due to Mick's storytelling technique. It applies to my job and I look forward to applying the concepts. I work as a supervisor in Information Technology. In IT, everybody treasures numbers and key performance indicators. Each week we turn in a status report full of numbers and lists. Starting this week, I plan to include at least one story each week in my status report that will communicate something we could change or improve.

- *David Ashlock*

Trust me I'm Human by Mick Mooney was an eye-opening book for me. Having been a teacher for many years, teaching 5 - 7 year old's, the concept of story telling was almost the only way information could be passed along. In fact, any subject could be made relatable this way. It was thus eye-opening to realise that this practice is so easily forgotten when we become adults. Mick not only provided a fresh take on this but made the concept and the application very relatable. Having read many of his other books I am reminded of Mick's own gift for storytelling.

- Elbie Kuhl

I absolutely loved this book! I think the topic/emphasis of storytelling is much needed in our world and Mick does a really good job of explaining why it's so important. No matter where you are in life, a mother; teacher; business leader; this book will enlighten you with the ability to connect powerfully with your children, colleagues etc. These human connections are essential for understanding; impacting; teamwork; and even love.

- Justin Cawoods

Mick Mooney has created a well-written, engaging book on the topic of engaging with other people to help drive change and focus on our core values. While the book is largely focused on the use of storytelling within an organisation, the usefulness of this material and strategy extends to practically any environment where you want to engage with other people.

I used this advice to revise a speech I was giving to my Toastmasters club a few days after reading the book, and the speech went over quite well. I will continue to use strategies from this book in a variety of business efforts (sales, consulting proposals and recommendations, motivation and leadership, etc.). I know I will be coming back to this book again, sometimes flipping through to catch my noted sections and sometimes to re-read in its entirety.

- Jeremy Weathers

This was a great book. The power of storytelling in business arenas, ministries, or anywhere that you are a leader. Every paragraph was impactful! Thank you Mick for writing such a thought-provoking book. I plan on implementing this with our board of directors, our employees and vendors, and our supporters. Powerful stuff!

- Lesa Jefferies

Loved this. I had been looking for a good book on leadership and then read this. Whilst its topics are broader than leadership, it really made me think about how I can introduce the concept of storytelling into our company to help instil our core values and improve internal communication. The book was so easy to read and has given me a bunch of actionable items.

- Tim Barnett

The power of a story has huge benefits! I know firsthand that storytelling connects people in an intimate and powerful way.

I'm an entrepreneur and have a few different businesses that are successful because of the stories that people hear about the modalities and the products used to get results. I have found, as Mick Mooney has laid out in this book, that it's really true that facts tell, but stories sell. Networking and connecting with people is what helps every business grow. Why not use storytelling to build and keep relationships? It really does work.

I love that Mick has used storytelling to let his audience know why storytelling works.

- Jane Bolen

If storytelling is an art, then we all need a teacher who can instruct us in the skills of being an artist. This guide can assist you to use the power of telling stories in a business environment. The various case studies show how telling stories takes courage and authenticity but can bring real benefits. As Mick says, "Storytelling is the greatest tool in an organisations communication toolkit. It will create magic where every other tool just passes on information. It will reach into the deeper, intuitive space within employee, the place where the inner hero lives, the place where they hear the call to adventure and respond". In this day and age, every organisation can do with a bit more magic!

- *Ruth McGowan*

TRUST ME, I'M HUMAN
WHY STORYTELLING WORKS AT WORK

BY MICK MOONEY

TABLE OF CONTENTS

Trust Me, I'm Human

"Storytelling is by far the most underrated skill in business"

Gary Vaynerchuk

Why Storytelling Works At Work

Joanne watched with concern as the next speaker began their presentation. Another financial report? Another jumbo-sized screen with a list of tiny bullet points? Was this the way GE Australia planned on kicking off the year? She could feel the disconnect, but that didn't stop each speaker from delivering one slide deck of data after the next.

Reluctantly, she turned and looked back from the front row and faced a sea of glazed over eyeballs. Their bodies were in the room, but their focus somewhere else entirely. The speakers were sharing content with the audience, but it wasn't enough. She knew things had to be different. They were going through the most significant transformation in the company's 125-year history and needed to drive seismic cultural change.

What the employees needed wasn't more information; it was to feel connected. They needed to be inspired by what GE was planning. They needed to feel the vision, not just hear about the technicalities.

When the leadership team debriefed later that week, Joanne spoke up:

"We can't run things like this again. It's not working. The staff are going back to their desks uninspired."

When pressed as to a better alternative, she said, "Let's tell stories instead. Not show data, but get staff to tell stories – invite them to present, and work with them to develop their storytelling skills. Let's empower the staff to share stories about what they've seen in the field, stories about the work they are doing that's making a difference in the lives of others; let's empower our staff to connect with one another, and bring across GE's vision in a more intuitively human way."

The leadership agreed, and Joanne was given the lead to turn their next kick off event into a storytelling one. That's what Joanne and her team did, flipping the roadshow on its head, renaming it GE Live, and focusing on employee storytelling.

Feedback from their debut storytelling event showed that 95% of employees said the stories they heard inspired them to win in tough markets, 95% of employees agreed that GE Live made them feel proud of their company, and 98% of employees agreed they would attend future events. All this happened with no traditional presentations and no data showcasing. It came through making storytelling the central mode of communication and bringing employees into the centre of those stories.

In the following weeks, emails continued to pour into Joanne and her team.

"Amazing stories from our employees; I was very proud of them and to be part of GE."

"Speakers were exceptional, each in their own way. The personal nature of their stories, delivered with genuine conviction was refreshing and different."

"Amazing speakers. The best I've ever seen in GE or at any event. Clear messaging, real stories and extremely well prepped to help bring out such amazing stories in just ten minutes each. Well done. We need to do more of this!"

It became clear to the leadership of GE that if they wanted to communicate their strategy effectively and to their employees they didn't need more data, they needed more genuine connection; the way to achieve that was through narrative, not numbers. They discovered the magic of connection was not created by the metrics they presented, but in the stories they shared.

Joanne is the VP of Communications for GE Australia and helps run TEDx Melbourne in her spare time. Talking with her about the changing world we live in, she brought all the complexity down to something simple and foundational: Connection. That's what we're really in danger of losing, and it's also what's most critical for businesses to keep hold of if they want to navigate the changing marketplace and consumer habits and expectations.

"We've fallen in love with things that can't love us back. We place more importance on phones than we do with each other," Joanne said. "Humans are designed to connect. It's how we learn and grow; without it, we don't have a process of discovery to create lasting perspectives. We end up in isolation, stuck in your own echo-chamber."

This is a problem that is slowly creeping into our lives. We are running the risk of losing the ability to truly connect with one another. I remember when I was growing up in the 80s the major technology every kid wanted was the little orange handheld game called Donkey Kong. If you were lucky enough to have it, you'd be glued to it at every opportunity.

I remember being dragged along to parties, to dinners, and on trips; it didn't matter where I was, if I had Donkey Kong I would be blissfully occupied. I would zone in on jumping rolling barrels and eating bananas. It also ensured I was disconnected from the world around me.

Fast forward 30 years. I was on the way to work and the bus was full of grown adults playing Donkey Kong. Well, that's what it looked like. These days we've replaced our kid game consoles for grown-up smartphones. And while they do keep us entertained, they are also keeping us disconnected.

LEADING WITH CONNECTION

The world has changed and with it effective leadership. The internet has open-sourced knowledge to the point it is now a commodity that anyone can access easily and freely.

The old saying 'knowledge is power' has become redundant, at least in context to leadership. In the past, a leader held great insights and knowledge in their heads, and it put them in a position of power. Now, even the most junior member of the team can access that knowledge within a few minutes of searching online. Great leaders, however, have always been set apart by their ability to connect with others. That has always defined great leadership, even if it's been overshadowed by the love of knowledge for a few hundred years.

With knowledge now an easily accessible commodity, the timeless truth that 'connection is power' is now being amplified more than ever before.

I like how Joanne explained it: "What's the difference between a leader today and Google? It's not knowledge; it's the ability to connect."

When you think about how we are wired as humans, it all comes back to stories. Storytelling is the oldest form of communication. Storytelling goes all the way back to the cavemen. Long before the spoken form of communication evolved, humans were already sharing stories. It's how we interpret *meaning*.

Due to the ancient and universal connection stories have to humanity, it's no surprise that stories move us emotionally where stats and facts never could. Stories are hard-wired into our human experience. Stories have a kind of secret key that can unlock parts of our inner thinking—including our beliefs and perceptions—that no other form of communication method can access.

Before the rise of the industrial revolution, humans—when they wanted to get attention, engagement and build authentic connections—communicated through stories almost exclusively. This is how trust was developed. It was how we evaluated authenticity. It was how we created a bond with one another. Information was passed on through narrative.

When the industrial revolution took place, narrative was replaced with numbers. When you are constructing buildings and bridges, and other mighty man-made wonders, numbers are very important. But the shift did more than just change the way we valued data. The industrial revolution effectively turned the majority of the workforce into robots, doing the same task over and over. In our modern marketplace, the artificial intelligence revolution is pushing us back to leverage our inherently human traits. The reason is simple. Humans make lousy robots compared to actual robots that are now entering the workforce.

So if we want to work with more of our human strengths, we need to tap into our more intuitive communication skillset: stories. We need to communicate with narrative because that's the way we truly connect, where we find an unspoken common ground, and where we build meaningful relationships—from there we can move forward in synergy and build meaningful projects together.

As humans, we love stories. We love them for entertainment, but on a deeper level we love them because they help us make sense of our own human experience. Stories resonate with us as individuals and build stronger bonds between us, too. The greatest invention of man was not the wheel, but the story, because stories have moved the human race forward more than all the wheels in the world.

Forbes recently called storytelling "the new strategic imperative of business" describing how it has now gained attention as a business competency that drives emotional engagement and results in enhanced business performance. This is the way business leaders need to think of storytelling; not as an artistic craft, but a *strategic* communication tool.

This book dives into what it means to be human, how we establish trust and connections with one another, and why storytelling is the most powerful strategy we can use to reach those outcomes.

"Tell me the facts and I'll learn. Tell me the truth and I'll believe. But tell me a story and it will live in my heart forever."

Native American proverb

VALUES &

LEADERSHIP

At the height of his popularity, Gandhi was travelling to a humanitarian conference with a delegation of westerners accompanying him. As he stepped onto the train, one of his shoes slipped off and fell into the gap between the platform and the train. Noticing he just lost a shoe, Gandhi reached down and took his other shoe off, tossing it into the gap before the doors closed. Eventually, one of the western delegates asked Gandhi why he just threw his shoe into the gap. Gandhi replied, "One shoe is of no use to me, but a poor man will find the pair on the tracks today and put them to good use."

When I heard this story, I had conflicted feelings. On one side I was inspired how it portrayed compassion, selflessness, consciousness, a spirit of unity, and character. I love all those values. On the other side, I found myself wondering if, given the situation, I would have done the same thing? I like to think like Gandhi, but would I have acted like him? I concluded, unfortunately, probably not.

Don't get me wrong, I would have loved to do it. It makes sense to do it. It's pointless not to do it. Gandhi was right; one shoe is of no value. The challenge is that there was only a few seconds between one shoe falling off and the doors closing. It was so fast; there wasn't any time to decide what to do. For Gandhi, it was instinct. To be honest, I think I would have spent those few seconds more in shock, or frustration, rather than in service to others, as Gandhi was.

We all have values we admire, we agree with, to which we aspire. But what does it take to have *lived* values? What does it take to have values that you live by so consistently and consciously, that it becomes instinct in the smallest of time frames?

Businesses all create corporate values. They are noble and right; they draw agreement from the staff; they are aspirational and inspiring—but are they lived? That's the challenge organisations need to address: How do we empower our staff to live our values, and not just agree with them?

What does it take for an organisation to truly live by its values?

That's the question I put to Swampy Marsh, Senior Director of Client Advocacy at Dimension Data. In particular, I was keen to get his thoughts on the whole topic of authentic leadership and the significance of self-awareness in the workplace.

"One of the core values of Dimension Data is integrity," Swampy shared early in our conversation. "What that means, in simple terms, is we do what is right to do. We don't compromise. I find integrity is often expressed in the small things in business. Telling the truth. Being open. Being transparent. Living up to our promises, and living out our company values."

So how does a large, complex organisation that spans dozens of countries make sure the small things get done well? After all, the small things seem to be the easiest things to do badly, to cover up, to forget altogether. What is the magic ingredient that makes it all work? Swampy believes it's authenticity. "Authenticity has to start within your executive leadership. For us, the focus is always on integrity and how we can make that an authentic value." I agree, authenticity is key, but it's hard to regulate authenticity, and that is where most companies get tripped up. They know they need it, but how to empower their staff to live it?

Authenticity reveals itself when leaders truly believe in the values of an organisation, so much so that those values find expression in everything they do, including the small things. In business, it's easy to go through the process of creating a strategic plan, or pulling together a smart-sounding vision, mission, and values board. But when they are treated as pieces of marketing collateral, used primarily to connect with the marketplace, leaders miss the great opportunity to give their strategy and values real life, and with real life comes real energy. It all comes back to authenticity.

It's safe to say that most companies want their staff to operate with genuine authenticity. The challenge is how to successfully embed this kind of culture into a business; Swampy understands that integrity as a core value can end up an empty shell. If he wants his staff to act with integrity the leadership at the top need to ensure their whole organisation is engaged in the vision, strategy, and values authentically, and kept accountable for it all. In short, they recognise they need a tactic that will activate such a strategic objective.

STORYTELLING BRINGS VALUES TO LIFE

One of best communication tools any leader can use to create more connection to the values of the organisation is storytelling. The story of Gandhi, as short as it is, helped me raise my consciousness about what my values were, and also increase my awareness of how I want to live those values. It also created an anchor point for discussing the theme with others. The same thing happens in business. Telling stories connects with a very deep part of our humanity. It's perhaps the only communication tool that breaks through the high defences and creates an opportunity to connect genuinely and openly. We often associate storytelling with entertainment, but on a deeper level, what it's associated with, is trust.

I was once running a storytelling workshop with a large telecommunications company. I shared a story about a prison in India with 170 inmates, each with a life sentence for murder. The walls around the compound were just two-foot tall. When you think of prisoners locked away for murder, two-foot walls don't come to mind. We think of 30-foot concrete walls, with barbed wire and armed guards on the lookout, but it's true. More amazing still is that the inmates are allowed to leave the prison at 6 am in the morning if they want to run their own businesses and work in the surrounding villages, which they all do. Because they are business owners and have the financial income to support their families, the prison also allows the families to live in prison. Essentially, the prison resembles a country village. Even though inmates could easily escape, there have only been a handful of escapes in 50 years, and there have been zero repeat offenders for murder.

The prison was inspired by the work of Mahatma Gandhi who believed everyone deserved a second chance, even murderers, and that family has central importance in one's life. The motto for the prison is: Trust begets trust. The prison is set up in a way that shows they trust the prisoners and in return, the prisoners prove that they are trustworthy.

I shared this story in the workshop to start a conversation about trust, asking, "What part of your organisation has 30-foot walls that can be brought down to two foot? What could you do as leaders to show your teams you trust them, and allow them the opportunity to prove that they are trustworthy?"

The story created a lively discussion that went on for about fifteen minutes. One of the participants shared some of the challenges he felt in bringing the 'walls' down and opened up about some of his previous life experience outside of his current work role. Afterwards, the team leader came up to me and said, "You know, I learned more about my colleague in that fifteen minutes than I have in the past ten years working with him."

It highlighted to me another powerful benefit of storytelling. People let their defences down, and they naturally feel more comfortable with sharing their thoughts, concerns, and personal connection to the theme that they would simply never share outside of a storytelling-led conversation.

STORYTELLING THAT EMPOWERS LEADERS

A few years ago Dimension Data made a strategic decision to put a focus on storytelling within their organisation and in particular with their senior leadership team. They ran formal and informal sessions on storytelling for business through their internal university, focused on how to use it effectively in a variety of business settings. It wasn't a marketing initiative; it was a communication initiative. They wanted to ensure senior leaders were given the insights and skills around using stories effectively in their roles. "To be honest, before the initiative I hadn't given too much conscious thought to storytelling," Swampy admitted. "But through the training, I became aware of my natural tendencies to use storytelling in my communications. So I recognised that I already valued it and actually used it a lot in business. I remember the training also helped create a beneficial dialogue between leaders, where we looked at projects and strategic plans and began asking what stories could be used to more effectively communicate them to our teams. Stories were already part of our natural leadership style, but the training helped us see it as a business tool, something tangible we could use consciously to improve our internal communications and also as a non-threatening way to talk about how we are living our values and ensuring we are working with integrity. Yes and no answers aren't very helpful in this regard, but sharing personal stories that reflect our shared values has proven to be very effective."

CREATING A CONNECTED CULTURE FROM TOP TO BOTTOM

Reena Malik is responsible for People Development at KPMG and works closely with her leadership team to implement people strategy throughout the organisation as well as building capability of professionals. As part of her role, she is focused on employee engagement and ensuring all staff members have a clear understanding of what KPMG stands for as a firm and how each employee plays a valuable part in KPMG's overarching purpose.

Reena travels extensively in her role, meeting with employees from across the globe; she's discovered that despite major cultural differences there are far more commonalities between employees. "At the end of the day, we are all human; we may be influenced by the cultures we grow up in, but we are defined by our humanity and that is where we all find common ground." Storytelling, regardless where she travels, remains the most effective way for Reena to help employees forge genuine connections.

"Storytelling brings everyone to a level playing field, from there we have a real chance of genuine connection. We want to create a culture that values people sharing their own stories and be encouraged by the stories of their coworkers." Reena knows how easy it is to inadvertently put leaders on a pedestal, presenting them as faultless; yet when we do that we also make them unapproachable. This pedestal-building happens by default when there are no stories being shared across the hierarchy of the business, and why being strategic with stories as an internal communication strategy is all the more important. We may admire our idols, but we identify with people's mistakes more than their successes; when someone has no mistakes, or they have no outlet to share their stories and expose the challenges they faced in the past and the mistakes they made, it's difficult for others to connect. Why is that? Because to make mistakes is to be human. To be hit with setbacks and to overcome those setbacks is to be human. And to tell stories of these experiences is to be human. It's why we love movies structured in the hero's journey format, not because the story of failure, setbacks and eventual overcoming is a great story, but because it is *our* story.

We are all heroes on a journey, and we must all own up to our mistakes and to continue despite our setbacks, and we all see in our future a victory we are destined to reach if only we can find our courage to fight for it. In our leaders in business, we are inspired not by their faultless list of accomplishments, but by their gritty patchwork of stories that tell the tale of mistakes and misfortunes, and through it breakthroughs and victories.

"Mistakes are part of being human and part of life," Reena explained. "Often people struggle to share those in the workplace, but it's those stories that help unite us. Part of my role involves bringing all levels of staff together, to understand each other, and find that common bond."

One of the ways KPMG is helping remove barriers and build

stronger connection across their organisation is through a program called Coffee with the Chairman. It's an initiative where the Chairman travels throughout the organisation and has a coffee with junior employees.

It's an informal meeting that seeks to create a campfire culture, an informal fireside-like chat where nothing is off limits to talk about, and questions can be asked within a casual conversation. These kind of meetings are designed to remove the invisible barriers junior and senior staff alike often create. It removes the sense of hierarchy and brings senior and junior employees to that great equal playing field, the unified human level, where talking about shared experiences and sharing their own stories about working at KPMG builds a genuine bond, one that can't be manufactured any other way.

Great company cultures are connected cultures. They can't be faked, but they can be forged through a willingness to be authentic, to own up to our humanity and to regularly share our stories of failures, ambitions, and victories.

CREATING AN ENVIRONMENT OF TRUST THROUGH STORYTELLING

The reason storytelling develops trust has a growing body of scientific backing behind its claims. Paul Zak is the founding director of the Center for Neuroeconomics. In 2004 he discovered the neurochemical behaviours of a chemical called oxytocin and how it creates a "safe to approach others" signal in the brain.

What has this to do with storytelling? A lot. When we hear a story that engages us, with it comes a surge of oxytocin. When this happens, our feeling of trust goes up, and our defences come down. It creates the environment for genuine connection. Oxytocin increases our sense of empathy for characters in a story, meaning an effective story induces the brain to make oxytocin, resulting in a strong emotional connection that overflows beyond the parameters of the story and into the relationship between the storyteller and the audience. In business and life, when we open up and make genuine connections, have honest conversations, and establish rapport, we experience progress and sow the seed of future transformation.

We can use our intelligence and data to craft our organisational values, but storytelling has the power to help everyone understand them, connect with them, discuss them with emotion, internalise them, and ultimately live them.

For storytelling to work, it can't be thought of as a task. It won't work its magic if it is treated as a one-off event. If you want your company values to be known and admired, hang them on the office walls; however, if you want them to be lived, then embed your values in relevant stories and share those stories regularly.

For storytelling to truly empower transformation, it needs to be a welcomed and nurtured part of an organisation's culture. When that happens, employees can embark on the journey from admiring company values, to truly living them.

HOW TO MAKE A SCIENTIST CRY

Paul travels extensively for work. A decade ago, around the time his team made their discoveries around oxytocin, he was travelling more than ever. He was also acutely aware his then young kids were waiting at home to play when he got home. He worked on flights, putting productivity above relaxation, so he could be present when he finally did get home. It was also an ideal time to work without distraction.

During one of those flights, they hit some major turbulence. The plane was bouncing around and the pilot explained it would, unfortunately, last most of the trip. He reluctantly packed away his laptop and switched on the in-flight entertainment.

A scientist primarily interested in the data, Paul rarely watched movies; however, he saw one of the movies (Million

Dollar Baby) had won a few Oscars and decided to watch it as a means of taking his mind of the turbulence.

Toward the end of the movie, the man next to Paul leaned over with a face of grave concern and asked if he was alright. Paul was in tears. Not just a few, he was a blubbering mess. The story had connected with him on such an emotional level that he cried uncontrollably. Paul's not small; he's 6,4 and usually a very rational, scientific type of guy. What happened was very unexpected.

So what did happen? Paul is a neuroscientist. He studies how and why the brain acts and reacts the way it does for a living, so on the way home he thought about the event from every angle. He knew the story wasn't real. He knew it was a Hollywood creation, and he knew the characters were professional actors. He knew all this rationally, so why did his brain respond as if it was all real? Why did the story have such an impact on him that although he knew the story wasn't real, his brain responded as if it was? It fascinated and disturbed him because he couldn't explain it.

He went back to the lab the next day and spoke to one of his partners, explaining what happened. Like any good scientists with a full lab at their disposal, they began running experiments on storytelling and its effect on the brain.

At the time they were still trying to discover what was the

way to stimulate and increase the creation of oxytocin in the brain. To their amazement, they found their answer in storytelling.

Not only did stories have the power to tap into people's emotions and create change in their brain activity, when stories were engaging, their research proved that stories also triggered the creation of oxytocin in a huge way. So big, in fact, that it changed the way Paul thought about his research, business, and purpose moving forward.

"Once we discovered that emotional stories are a more effective way of creating oxytocin, we kept experimenting, keep running tests and collecting data; the more we experimented the more it became clear that storytelling was the trigger we were looking for."

Paul is a scientist by training, but a storytelling-advocate as a result of his discoveries in the lab.

"What's driven my work as a neuroscientist has always come down to persuasion. I've always wanted to explain, through science, how people can more effectively persuade others to take action. It turned out that storytelling was the superpower I'd been looking for all along."

He's not the only one who believes storytelling is a superpower. The American Military once contracted Paul looking to give their troops a new superpower. They didn't want the latest AI drones or close combat martial arts training. They'd reviewed Paul's research and findings and decided to deploy a new form of training, storytelling training, that could empower their troops to negotiate and persuade others in hostile situations with words instead of guns.

Fewer guns and more stories in the world sounds like a winning strategy. In business, the same outcomes are just as desirable: less hostility, more collaboration, and a more desirable way to negotiate, persuade and engage. Storytelling in business is a superpower and a highly effective way of persuading people to take appropriate action.

"People do not buy goods and services. They buy relations, stories and magic."

Seth Godin

SALES &

DECISION MAKING

While writing this book I became hooked on watching the TV show Suits. If you don't know Suits, it's about a New York law firm. The main character is Harvey Specter, and he is a closer. He gets deals done. He never fails.

There's also another character, Louis Litt. He's a financial whizz, brilliant with the numbers, and the go-to guy when someone has to dig into the data and analyse it, but every time he tries to close a deal the whole thing goes pear-shaped. He's hopeless, and it's hard to watch because all he wants to do is impress Harvey; he wants to be like Harvey and be a closer. But Louis just isn't cut out to be a closer. Louis is exceptional with the numbers, but can't connect with people effectively. Harvey is disinterested in the numbers; he palms that kind of work off to his associate, but he's great at the communication piece. He knows how to reach the inner decision maker of every client.

Suits is just a show, but Louis and Harvey are everywhere.

Let's face it. Data is pretty lousy as a communication tool. It's a rockstar for *analysing* activity, but don't give it a mic. Don't ask it to get buy-in from others, or sell the concept to a prospect.

Data geeks out on the numbers, but don't think its genius with the numbers translates to it being a closer. It's not. It's incompetent at sales. It's embarrassing at getting buy-in to strategy.

It's a genius at analysing the *what*, but its hopeless at communicating the *why*.

Data is a tool for analysing. Stories are a tool for communicating *meaning*. Think about that. It's a big idea.

Data helps you come to the conclusion that you have something to sell (sell a product or sell a vision), it opens up the process, just make sure you don't ask it to close as well. Like Louis Litt, it's dismal at closing.

Stories are closers. They don't want to talk about the numbers. They don't even care about the numbers. Stories are not aiming for the head, they aim for the heart, for the gut, for the *emotions*. That's why they are closers. Because they know how decisions get made. Not with a person's rational thinking, but with a person's intuition, and intuition is linked to the heart, to the gut, and to their emotions. Once their intuition gives the green light, the head is left to write up the report and make it sound all business-like.

We know that decisions are made primarily through our emotions, and stories are the trigger to spark their emotions. The reality is that most of the time we make emotional decisions and then we use our rational thinking to create the justification for the decision. There's nothing wrong with that. It's part of being human too; what is important, however, is that we recognise this is what is happening and choose a communication strategy that is going to talk not just to the head, but to the emotions of others also.

Data is important. Let it do the research, analyse the situation, and set the deal up; just make sure you don't ask it to close for you, too. In Suits, when they needed a deal closed, they asked, "Where's Harvey?" In your business, when you want to close a deal, ask yourself, "Where's the story?"

SALESPEOPLE ARE AWESOME ... AND WE ARE ALL SALESPEOPLE

I remember the day my daughter made her first real sale. She was five years old. She had overheard my wife and I talking that morning about my day. I had a few meetings planned, and my wife asked, "Will it be a sales day?" I responded enthusiastically, "Yep, sales day." As it turned out, I did sign a new client to help him write, publish and promote his first business book; someone I have a huge amount of respect for who had a great story to tell. I texted my wife two words, "Sales day." My daughter, knowing the text was from Daddy, asked to read it.

When I got home my daughter was waiting at the door for me. She had a small basket full of toys with a handwritten note stuck on the front "sale, sale, sale". She begged me to take her out so she could have a sales day, too. The second 'prospect' (my hairdresser) bought a book from her. She was so excited about her first real sale. Back at home, I caught her in her room jumping up and down with her hands in the air chanting "Sales day, sales day, sales day!"

The next morning I was leaving for work when she smiled at me and asked, "Sales day today, Daddy?" I'd never been more motivated to make a sale in my whole life.

When I reflected on how that evening's events played out, I realised that I have always made a conscious effort to create a positive association with sales with my kids. The reason is simple. Sales is an awesome profession. The world is full of problems, and there are companies full of solutions—however, if they don't have salespeople to connect with those people how can they solve their problems? At the end of the day, that's what sales is: it's problem-solving. I want my daughter always to feel a sense of admiration for salespeople and to learn and develop her own skills in sales. She's already pretty good. What I love about it is she feels connected to sales in a positive way. That means her emotions are connected to the action, and the action is what brings about the result; the more results she gets and the more positive associations she makes, the better a salesperson (think: problem solver) she will become—and that's great because we are all salespeople. While going out and selling her toys was a one-off event, as a five-year-old she is undoubtedly trying to use her sales skills to close a lot of other deals at home. In my experience, kids are naturals at negotiation and seeking to close deals, it's a shame adults all too often try to knock these skills out of kids because they are skills that are so valuable when they grow up. No matter what profession my daughter goes into, she'll be a salesperson, because we are all salespeople. Daniel Pink's great book says it all in its title, To Sell Is Human.

> *"To sell well is to convince someone else to part with resources—not to deprive that person, but to leave him better off in the end."*
> *- Daniel Pink*

Selling is natural, it's needed, and it empowers solutions and a better future. The truth is we are all selling something if we have passion in our hearts and purpose in our bones. Maybe you're not selling in a traditional sense, where money is exchanged, but you're still selling something. You're selling ideas and ideals. You're selling perspective. You're selling a better version of life people can buy into. Great leaders are selling their *why* to their team every day; the teams that go on to change the world are the ones who first bought into their leader's vision. Every business is selling something, and for a good reason, because products and services solve problems; and for people with the very problem they are solving, that's good news. Without people selling, what would we have left? Just a lot of people weighed down with problems, with no solutions in sight and no vision for a better future.

Salespeople solve problems, but before they can do that they need to establish trust and a genuine connection with the very people who need their problems solved. Without a connection, people remain sceptical. It's not that they want to be sceptical, it's just that they don't feel the salesperson has their best intentions in mind. The key word there is *feel*. Buying anything is an emotional decision. Without the feeling, decisions get deferred. That's bad for everyone because it means problems stay problems.

Storytelling for salespeople is one of the most effective ways of building that connection, of creating a feeling in the buyer and moving people on an emotional level that in turn gets their decision making muscles involved.

It's one thing to want to solve someone's problem, but without creating that emotional connection, making that sale is always going to be tough. Perhaps that's why so many struggle with sales, because they're trying to sell with data? In contrast look at the best salespeople, what are they all about? Relationship, connection—and I bet if you followed them around you'd soon find out they were all about storytelling too. Why? Because stories are the primary way we as humans find meaning, connect emotionally, and make decisions. It's possible to increase the odds of success, and solve more problems in the process, by ensuring your conversations also include a good dose of storytelling.

HOW DECISIONS REALLY GET MADE

Neuroscientist Antonio Damasio made a groundbreaking discovery about how we as humans make decisions. As modern humans, we like the idea that we are rational beings when it comes to decision making. Damasio's findings turned this assumption on its head. His work revolved around studying individuals who had experienced damage to their brains, specifically to the part of the brain that generates emotions. These people could still function, they seemed unaffected physically by their injury; but they were affected, their particular kind of brain damage had resulted in them not being able to feel emotions.

His studies of this test group showed another unexpected commonality: they were unable to make decisions. It wasn't that they did not have the rational capability. In fact, they often would explain what they should do logically, but despite having the rational knowledge of what they should do, they could not bring themselves to make the decision. They would analyse the pros and cons, go over the facts and figures, recount rationally all the options and what seemed the best choice. Some decisions were large, but some were also about what kind of sandwich they should eat for lunch, chicken or turkey? Without their emotions to help them, they simply couldn't decide.

Damasio's findings highlighted just how important emotions are in the decision-making process, and considering business is all about persuading and empowering others to make decisions to purchase your product or service, it's a critical point that needs to be factored into any business strategy.

People don't make rational decisions. Their decisions are made primarily emotionally, and then they use their rational thinking to create the justification for the decision.

We have to remember that we are human, and, as humans, we develop trust through hearing and sharing stories; we also make decisions with our emotions, and storytelling hits our emotions better than any other form of communication.

DECISIONS ARE CRITICAL ORGANISATION-WIDE

Sure, you need prospects and clients to decide to buy your offer, but you also need your teams to decide to buy into your vision, you need them to decide to give whatever-it-takes to make your strategy succeed. You need the marketplace to decide your brand is trustworthy and worth keeping top-of-mind.

You also need your senior leaders to decide on the right strategy, not the safe one. You need stakeholders from all parts of the business to make decisions that move the organisation forward in harmony, rather than resisting decisions and instead creating an environment of stagnation and discord.

The most important thing in business is the ability to empower all stakeholders to make positive decisions that move the organisation forward.

If you want to know the real power of effectively using storytelling in business, it's this: *storytelling empowers decisions*. That's it. But considering that is the most important thing in business, it's more than enough.

But how exactly does storytelling empower decisions? We've discussed how it engages emotions and that emotions are a major driver of decisions, but it also hits on several other key attributes that lead to a decision being made.

FOCUS

The average goldfish has an attention span of nine seconds. Don't laugh, that's longer than the average Joe. According to a study from Microsoft in 2015, people now generally lose concentration after eight seconds, highlighting the effects of an increasingly digitalised lifestyle on the brain.

Storytelling combats this for a simple reason. Stories have a beginning, middle, and end. In other words, stories are a narrative that from second to second are moving forward.

This keeps the brain's attention because it becomes curious and must stay focused if it is to follow along. Compare this to showing a range of statistics and then speaking about them. This is not a second-by-second narrative, but rather an information dump—so, in this scenario, after eight seconds guess what happens? The mind finds a more interesting rabbit hole to venture down.

By telling stories, you allow people's brains to lock in and follow, knowing that stories have a payoff at the end; the climax, the reveal, the insight.

If you want people to remain focused, don't front-load the insights; rather, tell a story that exemplifies the insight first, and tag the insights on at the end when their focus is high.

TRUST

The more people are in the mindset of analysis, the more they want to find fault. It's the nature of analysis. The old saying 'paralysis by analysis' is true. The more we analyse, the less we are capable of making a decision. So why would you want to lead with data? Why put your listener intentionally into analysis mode? A far more effective communication strategy is to lead with a story that embodies the essence of the data, without actually running through the data.

Science backs this up as well. As I mentioned in the

previous chapter, when we tell and hear stories, our brains begin to create a chemical called oxytocin. Other times oxytocin is activated is when we are around people we love, and when we hug people. It has been called the Trust Hormone because when it is activated our defences are automatically reduced and our levels of trust increase. This has the opposite effect of statistics. When we are presented with statistics our brains boost the defences because we become unsure, we have to suddenly compute new data, and we don't have time to analyse the result, so we become more guarded. By having a storytelling strategy and leading with stories, you can empower your listener to lower their defences and trust you more, all which are critical if you want to empower them to make a positive decision.

AGREEMENT

If you want people to make decisions, you need first to help them feel you are both in agreement. In agreement with what? With everything. Legendary sales trainer Grant Cardone once told me that agreeing with your prospect is one of the most critically important elements of the sales process. I believe him. In fact, if you get this wrong, you will unlikely get the sale at the end. It's serious stuff.

One of the ways to get agreement that is not verbal, but just as powerful, is through storytelling. The reason for this has to do with our DNA. Since the stone age, we have communicated almost solely through stories. It is only in the last few hundred years of the industrial revolution that we began communicating by data. In other words, we are hardwired to communicate and interpret meaning intuitively through stories, but data still requires manual, conscious brain work. Our brains like to be lazy; in fact, they need to be. They are constantly looking for ways to conserve energy. So if you want it to work hard, you need to have to give it a really strong motivation. Most of the time, your listeners (team members, prospects, stakeholders) aren't going to have that strong a motivation, so rather than try to get agreement via their rational thinking, go for it through their intuitive thinking. When you tell stories, it activates focus, it establishes trust, and through stories you are transferring meaning through emotion, so the brain doesn't have to put in the work to interpret data (which most people just don't want to do because it takes concentrated effort). Through the telling of stories, your hearers can intuitively understand your point and agree with it with much less effort and greater interest.

Throughout the time it takes to tell a short story, your listener may have come into agreement with you several times. Not on a head level, but on a more instinctive level. It's all the same, though. The more agreement you have, the greater the chances they will make a rational, verbal agreement later in the meeting.

If empowering people to make decisions is what you want to do; being of great service, solving problems, and creating a solution-based future is why you want to do it; storytelling is how you should communicate.

If the most important thing in business is the capacity to empower a range of stakeholders to make a decision, then you have to take seriously a storytelling strategy. It's not just an interesting way to communicate; it's a strategic way; it's the way you increase the level of positive decisions that get made.

"Storytelling is the most powerful way to put ideas into the world today."

Robert McKee

Presentations
& Purpose

In Suits, there's a great scene where Harvey walks into a meeting with a prospective client. The man looks up at Harvey and his first blunt question is, "Where's your PowerPoint presentation?"

Harvey responds with a smile, "I don't need a PowerPoint presentation."

The potential client is somewhat confused by this and asks Harvey why he thinks he doesn't need one when all the other firms he's met with had one. Harvey answers it's because he knows what the potential client wants—loyalty. As soon as he says this the guy drops his guard and replies, "You're right."

What did Harvey come into that meeting with? It wasn't a PowerPoint presentation; it was something far more powerful —he came in with *clarity*.

The scene highlights an important reality that people don't want information; they want clarity. If you can give them that, they'll drop their guard and listen, connect, and engage.

WHAT'S THE POINT OF STORYTELLING IN BUSINESS?

The fish gets bigger at each telling of the story. Soon enough, it wasn't a tuna Jack's grandfather caught, it was a shark; no, wait, it was a whale! Yes, a blue whale, have you ever seen one of those? Can you imagine it? Ol' grandpa caught one in his dingy and a bit of fishing line. Nobody'd ever seen anything like it. A toast to grandpa, who caught a blue whale off the ferry on the way to work with nothing but a shoestring and some sticky tape. What a guy!

You've been there before, right? You're at a party, and a crowd has formed around someone telling a whale of a story, it's epic, it's funny, it's got you on the hook . . . but it's not exactly the truth. Afterwards, you thank the storyteller for the entertainment—and ask if the story was completely accurate. The response? A slap on the back, a warm, honest laugh, and the age-old advice from veteran storytellers, "Never let the facts get in the way of a good story."

When you're recounting stories at parties or around the campfire, it's OK to be a bit fishy on your facts.

IT ALL COMES DOWN TO PURPOSE

What's the purpose of telling the story? If you're at a party with friends where everyone is simply looking to unwind and have a bit of a laugh, and telling a story is for pure entertainment value, then fudging some facts to make the story more entertaining is standard (mal)practice. Filmmakers also tell stories for entertainment, so it's OK to create a modern day dinosaur park and pass it off as plausible because the point is not to be factual, but entertaining.

The same 'purpose' rule applies when telling stories in business. What is the purpose of telling the story in a business setting? And here is where things differ significantly. The purpose of telling a story in business is never for entertainment (although it can be entertaining, and should be entertaining if possible, being entertaining is not the point of the story). Unless it's a purely social situation, there should always be a business objective behind the story.

NEVER LET A STORY GET IN THE WAY OF GOOD FACTS

The purpose of storytelling in business is to help an audience understand a meaning clearly, and internalise it so it can be remembered and acted upon. Pushing important facts and figures onto them alone doesn't work for several reasons. First, it's not that easy to understand new information, so while people might nod along, it's unlikely they understand; and if they don't understand, then they are not clear on your point, and that means they are not internalising anything you're sharing, and they won't remember much either.

This is why the power of storytelling in business matters. It's the stories you tell that make all the difference in the success of your communication because unlike new information, stories don't have to be interpreted intellectually. They get interpreted by emotion; because, as humans, we are experts at interpreting things by our emotions on the spot, we can understand the point of a story almost instinctively; and when we understand we become clear on your point, and that means we have already started internalising what you're sharing, and we'll remember the story afterwards, too.

So it's important your story is not just entertaining, but it is embedded with the purpose of your facts and figures that you want to pass on; not in bullet point form and tiny font, but distilled down to make the point clear. It's not narrative or numbers. It's both.

Storytelling in business should never compete with data. They are a team. Stories and data: it's Harvey & Louis, an odd yet somehow effective team. However, it is essential to understand the different roles data and stories play. Don't ask Harvey to crunch the numbers and don't ask Louis to win new clients.

PRESENTING WITH EMOTION AND LIFE

You've been there before. Sometimes as the victim, sometimes as the Bullet-Point Assassin. You know people are not engaging. It's not a guess. You know it, but what can you do? The only thing one can do—click the button and move to the next slide.

But why do we do it? That is the real question. Why do we think it is a good idea, a smart business decision, to cram ten bullet points onto a slide, the read out all ten points verbatim? Why do we put people through it; more perplexing, why do we put ourselves through it? After all, we created the slides. The presentation was in our hands to craft, and nobody said you had to kill the audience with data, did they? The goal was to present *what* exactly?

And therein lies the problem. Often, we're not clear on the specific point of the presentation. We might know the data, but what about the purpose?

I've noticed that those that understand the purpose, rarely present data; rather, they embed the purpose within a story or several stories. Often people focus on the art of storytelling and self-disqualify themselves by saying, "Oh, I'm not a storyteller." But I would challenge you not to think about it as a stand-alone skill that you can reject or embrace, but as a vehicle to transfer ownership of ideas. It is a framework to communicate purpose. It's not about if you are a good storyteller, but if you know the purpose of your presentation.

Next time, when you are at the starting point of preparing for a presentation, rather than rush into compiling data, stop and ask yourself: What is the purpose of this presentation? What big idea do I want my audience to take ownership of? What is the value I want to communicate?

From there, think about what stories you know, either from personal experience or from someone else's experience that will communicate that purpose, that big idea, without the need for bullet points. Stories are great because they don't spell-it-out-with-data, and thus avoid activating the snooze button in the audience's brain almost immediately; rather, a story will keep the audience engaged as they begin to make sense of the story as it is being told, and remain engaged as they wait with expectation for the resolution of the story and the inevitable learning payoff at the end.

Without first being clear on what outcome you want from the presentation, and specifically what idea you want to transfer to the audience, the default strategy seems to be to put them to sleep with fifty slides of small font detail. Sure, you can stick in a few images, but bullet points with sugar on top are still snooze-mode for an audience. Rather, make it your ambition to communicate your message through engaging your audience with a compelling story that makes the point you desire.

Nobody wants to find themselves behind closed doors in a dark room with a Bullet-Point Assassin; but a compelling storyteller that's engaging and ultimately delivers greater outcomes is warmly welcomed.

The world needs more storytellers in business. Not because we need more stories, but because we need more leaders who have enough *clarity* behind their purpose to lay aside the bullet points and instead paint the picture, frame the adventure, and invite us into the experience.

Tell someone the facts and they'll nod in agreement, then leave the room and forget what they were even nodding about. Tell them a story that embodies the facts and they'll become an advocate on your behalf, getting all the other decision makers—who weren't in the room—into agreement for you. Facts and figures don't win you the work, stories do. Send your audience the facts via email straight after the presentation, but when you have people in front of you, devote the time to telling a compelling story that captures the essence of what your facts and figures are actually about. Bring life, colour, laughter, and intrigue back into the boardroom. Be a storyteller.

HOW STORYTELLING PREPARES A LEADER TO COMMUNICATE EFFECTIVELY

It helps to think of storytelling as a communication tool used to prepare a leader to communicate effectively, rather than a tactic to throw into the mix.

- **Meaning:** *You have to figure out the point of your communication in advance. It's impossible to craft a compelling story to make your point if you don't know what the point is.*

- **Purpose:** *You have to figure out what is in it for the audience you will be communicating with. If you don't know the reason they should* *listen, you won't find the story to facilitate keeping their attention.*

- **Outcome:** *You have to figure out what outcome you want before you can craft a story to lead people to that outcome.*

Using storytelling as a preparation tool is about clarity. Storytellers have the edge over all other leaders, because of the clarity they get in the preparation stage of forming their stories for their meetings and presentations.

When stories are then included in a presentation, the preparation is what empowers the moment of connection with the audience and team members, and facilitates the opportunity for ongoing transformation.

Storytelling doesn't just give a leader the edge when they are in the spotlight; it gives them the edge in their preparation too. Becoming a storytelling leader is a strategic decision, not an artistic one

Storytelling isn't a marketing thing; it's a human thing. It's a communication tool. It can be leveraged to reach your audience on an emotional level; it's about building a connection, it's about creating focus within a team; it's about creating a lasting memory.

For the leaders who take it seriously, storytelling also creates clarity—that's important because clarity that can be communicated and shared effectively is ultimately what facilitates future growth and transformation.

THE SUCCESS OF TED TALKS

With over a billion views to their videos, it's worth exploring what makes TED presentations so appealing? One of the main reasons is that TED talks make the audience feel smart, rather than showcase how smart the presenter is. They do that through making storytelling the almost exclusive way of presenting. There are many deep thinkers who give TED talks, including some of the brightest academic minds on the planet. These experts, however, don't use TED to showcase the depths of their knowledge—they don't have time to do that. Each speaker gets just 18 minutes. This limited time restriction is a stroke of genius because it ensures presenters know the one point they want to make, not the hundred and one points they could talk about for days on end—just one.

This time restriction helps their presenters get laser-focused on the purpose of their presentation. But it is not just getting clear on the point and purpose of the presentation; it's also ensuring the presenters make a meaningful and lasting connection with the audience. To do that, they are not allowed to present facts and figures or an array of bullet points on the big screen; rather, they have to embed their facts and figures in a story. It is storytelling that is the ultimate framework for TED talks, and it has quietly created a revolution in how we present in business.

TED taps into the human instinct to gravitate towards stories, to lean in, to listen, to let our left brain guard down and surrender to wonder. In the process, to learn, to grow, to appreciate, to connect.

The revolution shouldn't end in how we run presentations. The same elements that make TED so effective and successful can work in all areas of business. It's not the brand TED that makes it work, but the method it uses; namely, storytelling.

THE POWER OF A STORYTELLING CULTURE

Joanne Woo spends a lot of her time coaching the presenters for their annual TEDx Melbourne conference, an independently run TED conference; most of the time the presenters invited are not professional speakers. Rather, they are simply people with an idea worth spreading. Joanne and her team help make that happen by coaching presenters over a six month period on the lead up to the big event in the method of TED: They help them get clear, find the right stories, and create a presentation that is not scripted, yet very purposeful; they help their presenters share their ideas in a way that gives them the best chance of spreading.

Joanne enjoys the contrast between her leadership role at GE and her TEDx role. "I've met the most extraordinary people through TED; there's so much diversity and a great spirit of inclusion. Everyone wants to learn and grow; ideas and stories have a way of bringing people together. One of the reason's I joined TEDx was just for that. In a corporate setting it's easy for people to play it safe and stick to the status quo, resulting in having the same conversations about the same ideas with the same kind of people; GE is really progressive in the area of ideas (they did create the light bulb, after all) but I wanted to make sure I wasn't just stuck in my own echo-chamber. TEDx helped me see how much power there is in a storytelling culture that embraces and promotes ideas and naturally creates diversity and inspires conversation long after talks have ended. I love that I can bring some of the TEDx magic back into my workplace; every time we run a TEDx I come back to work incredibly inspired and ready to apply those lessons learned in a professional setting. The power of storytelling is something I want to embed in the heart of all we do at GE because the outcomes are so empowering and beneficial."

"When you begin to talk in stories, your black-and-white words turn into colour. Your drab requests turn into mission. People find you to be more compelling; and once that happens, others will see that stories work, and they'll start telling stories, too."

Annette Simmons

CUSTOMER

EXPERIENCE,

CLARITY & CULTURE

I recently had to accompany my daughter to a birthday party. It was the first time I didn't have to stay at the party; instead, the hosts advised me the kids were fine and to come back in 90 minutes. The problem was I had nowhere to go. I didn't live close by so I decided to go to the RSL[1] next door.

I walked to the bar and waited a minute or so for someone to

---

1   RSL stands for Returned and Services League. It is an Australian support organisation for men and women who have served or are serving in the Defence Force, but is open to the whole community for drinking, dining and entertainment.

serve me and ordered a green tea. The bartender looked at me funny, expecting me to rather order a beer, then bounced around the bar looking for the teabags. When she found it, she put it in a mug, filled it with hot water and handed it to me. I went to pay, but she waved me away, telling me not to worry about it, "After all," she said, "It's just a mug of water and a tea bag."

I took my tea and sat down, and was somewhat puzzled because in my mind I wasn't buying some water and a tea bag. I was buying the experience. That meant I was buying the comfortable furniture, the air conditioning, the quiet place to sit and read; I was buying the convenience—and yes, I was buying the water and the teabag.

The problem the bartender had was she did not understand or appreciate what the RSL's customer experience actually was. It wasn't about beer or any other product they served—it was about the more significant experience. But the bartender only saw two feet in front of her, she saw the teabag and water and that was it; because of this, she thought I was purchasing the commodity, and in her mind, the commodity was not worth much, in fact she actually thought it was worthless.

The truth is I would have happily paid a premium price for the tea if it meant I could enjoy the experience of the RSL as a whole for 45 minutes. But the employee who served me just didn't get that. I don't think she's alone. In too many businesses the leadership fail to empower the staff to truly understand, grasp, and value the customer experience they are creating, not just the end product.

THE IMPORTANCE OF CUSTOMER EXPERIENCE TO BE REAL AND CONSISTENTLY DELIVERED

A recent Walker research paper reports that by 2020 Customer Experience (CX) will overtake Price and Product as the key brand differentiator in the marketplace. That's huge. This is a major shift in the business world, and forward-thinking organisations are already aligning, or in the process of aligning their strategy to reflect the central importance of CX. But with this shift in strategic focus comes some challenges that every organisation needs to overcome.

 This is all great news for the consumer and the marketplace if it works. And that's a big if, because a lot of organisations fail to make the concept of the Customer Experience understood by the very people who are an integral part in delivering it: the staff.

 Organisational-wide buy-in is critical, but so often it fails to happen. Why? What's the roadblock? What would cause an organisation to fail to live up to their grand aspirations? I believe it again comes down to one word: *clarity.*

It's not enough for the leadership team to know what the ideal experience should be. The entire organisation needs to believe and see the value in the experience. The bartender in the RSL didn't have any clarity on the desired experience; even though it was a nice experience and the RSL obviously put a lot of thought and effort into creating it, their employees didn't have a clear vision of that experience. If they are not clear on what the experience is, then how can they be part of successfully facilitating that experience? It brings it all down to chance, and no organisation can afford that.

HOW TO GET EMPLOYEES TO TRULY UNDERSTAND THE CUSTOMER EXPERIENCE

If you want your Customer Experience strategy to work, one of the easiest and most cost-effective ways to do that is to layer it with a storytelling strategy. This is the critical piece that unfortunately only a few get. The reason it is so essential is that at its core, storytelling requires clarity first. You can't build a compelling story without first having a clear understanding of the narrative you want to share. So from a leadership perspective, the exercise will force the group to get to the point of real clarity before they can even begin to shape some stories to exemplify it. That's already a significant result. In fact, this alone makes the whole storytelling component of the strategy extremely helpful. It makes sure there's real clarity that can be simply expressed (not just business mumbo-jumbo) before things progress further.

It's the organisations that create a series of narratives that breakdown and make their CX emotionally tangible that manage to provide it consistently. Without a narrative based way of teaching and clarifying the CX with staff, there is a danger of it remaining a lofty concept on an executive level, yet foggy and misunderstood on the ground. What does the CX look like and feel like from end to end, from intention to outcome, from team to team, from location to location? Explaining the CX won't make it stick, you have to bring it to life through a series of compelling stories.

CREATING MINI STORIES TO TEACH, GIVE CLARITY, AND AFFIRM THE CUSTOMER EXPERIENCE

The RSL could have created several narratives (mini-stories) around each part of the Customer Experience, from walking in the doors, to the music that's playing, to the sense of calm and relaxation, to the choice of food and drinks and so on; these stories can be linked together to then give an overarching story of the Customer Experience, but can also be used as stand-alone stories when training or talking about a specific part of their Customer Experience.

Once these sets of stories are created, they can be of enormous value to any leader in the organisation seeking to explain and reaffirm the Customer Experience of the company. Without stories to paint the picture and raise awareness, and respect for the overall value and reasoning behind the CX, employees think all they're selling customers is the end product, the commodity, the *thing*. Stories told to deliver clarity, awareness, and inspiration are what empower employees to realise what they are delivering to the customer: not just the commodity but of greater worth, the *experience*.

The reality is this: regardless of the business we are in, what we are all selling is the Customer Experience. That's what customers want (not the tea bag and hot water) that's what brings them back, and that's what makes them raving fans... it's also what they will happily pay a premium for.

"The most powerful person in the world is the storyteller. The storyteller sets the vision, values and agenda of an entire generation that is to come."

- Steve Jobs

If you struggle to get clarity in your business, rather than get analytical and break out the project management software and Excel spreadsheet, sit down and give storytelling a go because it's the only way you can share a complicated process (whatever your strategy is) in a simple and powerful form of communication. It's also an effective way to address the possible elephant in the room (and the elephant in the room is almost always a clarity problem).

Sending around a detailed strategic plan with numbers and objectives won't achieve much. But if you can capture your team's attention and imagination through a compelling story that explains the core of your strategy, you'll win in the marketplace. It's a big claim but look around at who's winning in the marketplace. They all have storytelling cultures.

HOW EMPIRES ARE BUILT

Richard was trying to get out of the city. He was at the airport waiting patiently for his plane when it was announced the flight had been cancelled. His girlfriend was already at the holiday resort on the British Virgin Islands. She would be waiting for him to arrive.

Despite the cries of all the passengers, they were told there were no more flights and to go home; but Richard was desperate. He wanted to get to his girlfriend. He wanted to start his holiday. Instead of getting frustrated, he got radically creative.

Within minutes of the plane originally being cancelled, Richard had approached the airline and convinced them to charter him an entire plane. He had to get to his girlfriend regardless of the costs. Not wanting to leave others stranded when he now had a whole empty plane to take him to the same destination they wanted to get to, he made them an offer. Richard borrowed a blackboard and scribbled on it:

"Virgin Airlines: £39 one way to BVI"

He filled the plane.

It was the first official Virgin airlines flight.

Later that week he called Boeing to ask how much it cost to buy a plane, just out of curiosity; the rest is history.

How many times do you think Richard Branson has told that story? I bet he's lost count, and every time he tells it, I'm equally sure he enjoys the tale as if it was the first time sharing it. Why? Because it's genuine, it's fun, it's bold; it's also a great way to communicate the kind of business Virgin is: innovative, embracing, courageous, and different.

Today Virgin is one of the most innovative and successful

companies in the world, with an ability to move into almost any industry. It's no surprise it also has a very purposeful storytelling culture. In fact, they take it so seriously they spent the whole month of March specifically devoted to highlighting the importance of storytelling and creating events and opportunities for employees to share their stories. Branson goes as far as attributing his success to storytelling. It's a big deal, but not for the gimmick and eyeballs it gets on the brand; Branson understands storytelling is a deeply human way of communicating and connecting; it doesn't just work when marketing your brand, it also creates a culture that attracts and retains the best talent available. Storytelling is essential for all marketers looking to get attention on and offline, but it's a mistake to think of storytelling as a marketing thing. It's a human thing, and businesses are filled with people who will ultimately make or break the company.

It's beneficial to create a campfire culture; it's not just a fun idea, it's a strategic way to build an agile, connected, and trusting culture.

THE CAMPFIRE CULTURE

Sitting around the campfire telling stories is an ancient tradition; its origins go back to when mankind first discovered fire. But the world was a dangerous place back then and has been for most of mankind's history. That meant that for most of the time, people needed to be on guard, they needed to be prepared to run, or fight, or defend themselves. Because of this, the campfire became a signal that things were safe. If they were around the campfire, it meant some of the tribe were standing guard, out in the darkness, protecting their camp. It meant inside the camp was safe, that they could let their guards down, relax, and enjoy each others company. The campfire symbolised it was time to connect and enjoy the best part of being human.

It was around the campfire that stories were told. Stories of the tribe's heroes and gods. Stories of the day's activities. Stories of memories they held. Stories that reinforced the tribe's connection. Stories that inspired and intrigued. Stories that made them feel a whole range of emotions.

The campfire is metaphorical in today's day and age, when we tell stories, it still triggers that part of the brain that says, "OK, this is a safe time, I can let my guards down, I can connect." Paul Zak discovered and documented the science behind oxytocin, the Trust Hormone, and how it is created in the brain when a story is told. The science is clear and detailed, but if you want a simple picture of what creates oxytocin, think of the campfire.

For most of us, the campfire is a useful metaphor to

understand how our brains have evolved over thousands of generations to trust people and connect with stories, but Branson still uses the campfire in a literal sense, believing it is a core part of not just building connection, but building a business as well. Considering he's one of the most successful and loved entrepreneurs in the world, it's beneficial to learn from him.

Most evenings, on Richard Branson's Necker Island, end with family, friends, and guests sitting around a campfire sharing about their lives, their passions, their business; it's a place to share their tales and adventures, their experiences and beliefs; it's a place to connect on a very human level. It's the time they tell each other their authentic stories. Many of the guests are business people, but on the island, they are all considered part of the tribe, and around the campfire, everyone can be trusted, included, and encouraged.

In an age of rapid change and disruption, being agile and innovative is critical. So is sharing thoughts and ideas about change and what's possible. Branson believes telling stories within his team, whether that is around Necker's campfire or in a meeting room downtown, is one of the best ways to come up with new ideas and also a powerful way of learning about each other and our world.

"Humans are not ideally set up to understand logic; they are ideally set up to understand stories."

Roger C. Schank

CHANGE &
TRANSFORMATION

After a decade-long struggle to get into the city of Troy, the ancient Greek army was ready to up and leave in defeat. They had tried all the strategies of force that had worked in the past with no result. They had laid siege to the city for years, and it didn't seem to bother the inhabitants inside the walls in the least. They needed to get inside those city walls, but how?

Instead of force, they decided to try one more strategy.

They constructed a large wooden, beautifully crafted horse. Under the leadership of Epeius, the Greeks built the wooden horse in three days. They put an inscription on it that read:

"For their return home, the Greeks dedicate this offering to Athena."

They packed a selection of their best fighting men inside the horse, and put the rest of their armies on their boats and left, disappearing over the horizon.

The leaders of Troy, watching the ships leave, came out of their walls celebrating. They saw the horse, read the inscription, and rejoiced. The Greeks had given up and retreated, leaving behind an offering to the gods. They wheeled the giant horse into their city centre as a sign of victory for all the citizens.

That night, the men slipped out of the horse and opened the gates to the city. At the same time, the Greek ships had returned under cover of night and the army effortlessly entered Troy—because the gates were now wide open.

THE POWER OF FEELING AN EXPERIENCE

Everyone was buzzing with excitement. The small ten seater plane was buzzing too. It was noisy—until we began flying over the Grand Canyon. Suddenly, everyone stopped talking. It felt like the engines even switched to silent mode.

I'd never seen anything like it. No one had. We had nothing to compare it to. We gazed out of the windows in silent fascination. A few minutes later we landed and exited the plane.

I was with three of my best friends on a trip around the world. A tour of the Grand Canyon was a last minute inclusion in our itinerary; although close to twenty years ago, it remains to be one of the most lasting memories I have.

The first thing I said to one of my friends as we stood gazing over the unfenced edge of the Grand Canyon was, "Nobody will understand this. It doesn't matter how many pictures we take; they won't get it unless they come here and experience it for themselves."

There were a lot of canyons on the way to the Grand Canyon. They were certainly impressive in their own right, but they didn't create the same reaction in me. It was as if I could appreciate the canyons on a rational level, but the Grand Canyon moved me in a deeper way; it connected with me on an emotional level, and that's what made my experience so different, so inspiring, so memorable.

Transformational communication is like the Grand Canyon; it imparts an emotional reaction. When I look at my photos of the Grand Canyon, I don't have the same feeling like when I was actually there, when I was experiencing it. But how do you bring people into that kind of experience without literally transporting them there?

CREATING ROUND HOLES FOR ROUND PEGS

My son has a love-hate relationship with one of his toys. It's a simple game with a square peg, a round peg, and a triangle peg. There is also a wooden box, and on the top is a square hole, a round hole, and a triangle hole. The goal, of course, is to put the pegs into their corresponding holes. To a grown-up, this seems like a straightforward task, but to a toddler it's incredibly perplexing. My son tries to fit the round peg into the square hole, and when it doesn't fit he lifts it up, pauses a moment, and then tries again. To his surprise, it still doesn't fit. Despite the lack of success, he doesn't try another hole; instead, he doubles down on trying to fit the round peg into that stubborn square hole.

When it comes to communication, all too often we make the same mistake. We focus on our round peg, not on the audience's square hole. We have a round peg (new idea, new project, new deadlines, new direction), but we fail to realise the audience has a different shaped hole (my life, my security, my skills, my ideas); no matter how great, important, and transformational our information seems to us, it simply won't fit. The result is failed communication. If your message doesn't 'fit' the audience, then your important information and suggestions will likely bounce off them. The reason is obvious, but that doesn't mean we naturally get it; as my young son has yet to learn, round pegs don't fit into square holes, regardless of the force applied.

The solution is not to change your round peg; instead, it's to help your audience change their square hole. But how do you do it?

Rather than tell them the facts, tell them a story instead. One element of storytelling that is very powerful is it gets focus and engagement before the audience knows where the story is ultimately going. They must tune-in, connect, and follow along to understand the story and its ultimate meaning. Alternatively, if you start with the data, the audience immediately judges what they assume you are getting at (change, risk, more bad management decisions, more wasted time, more work, less pay) and begin to build their fortress of resistance while you continue breaking down the details.

It helps to take time to get clear on what the ultimate payoff for the audience will be (what's in it for them) and what the ultimate payoff for others will be (how are we going to change the world). When you can express these points within a compelling, authentic story, you can draw their attention into the narrative, giving them time to come to their own conclusions, updating their initial perceptions, and changing the way they will receive the information that follows. If you can get clarity first, you can get engagement later. A story told effectively can go before your information, change the shape of the peg hole, and then give you the platform to communicate more effectively and with greater receptivity.

Stories can turn a square hole into a round hole; they can move the mindset of your audience to go from resistant to receptive to your new ideas, from critical to curious, from disengaged to intrigued.

My toddler just keeps banging that round peg at that square hole. Hopefully, when he grows up he won't choose that same strategy in business too. There's a better way to communicate in business to get far more effective outcomes. If what you really need is buy-in, engagement, and collaboration, don't force the numbers to the front; lead with a narrative, pull them into a story they want to play a part in, and then explain how they can do just that.

The goal is to shift your focus from what you want people to accept (your round peg) to how you can empower people to create a new way in their thinking before you attempt to communicate your change requirements. You need to enable your audience to change their perspective before they accept direction on changing their actions. To do this successfully you need a Trojan Horse strategy because you can't help people create a new thought processes and aligned desires from outside their fortresses, but you can once you are on the inside.

HOW TO 'SHARE' AN EXPERIENCE

Uri Hasson is a neuroscientist based at Princeton University who researches the neurological basis of human communication and storytelling. His lab experiments have revealed some fascinating effects storytelling has on the brain. In one study Uli and his team had five people sit and listen to the same story. These people were hooked up so the scientists could monitor their brain function throughout the experiment. Before the story started everyone's brain activity was different. However, when the story started something changed in all their brain activity—they all became synced. While listening to the story, their brain activity was the same.

 Hasson and his team took his research further, experimenting with storytelling on the brain when it came to retelling stories. What they found was fascinating. Not only did a person's brain align to the storyteller's brain, sparking the emotional experience of the story, but when they then went out and retold the story to someone else, the same effect happened. This showcases the extraordinary power of stories to communicate more than information; they can transfer the emotions of the story's experience also. Stories are the perfect tool for those who want to be transformative communicators.

This is known as neuro-coupling, a phenomenon whereby two or more people's brain activity synchronises, coming into alignment with their thoughts and emotions. This happens when people hear a story that is authentic and emotional. When it comes to change management and organisational transformation, creating an environment where neuro-coupling can take place can be a game-changer. This is where storytelling as a strategy begins to make clear business sense. In the moments employees are seeking to disengage and seek their self-preservation, you can draw them back into engagement, but not just engagement with the business, but with each other as well.

Storytelling done right can be a catalyst for creating organisational-wide synergy. It can move people from disengaged and defensive to engaged and courageous; it is a strategy to achieve what seems impossible. It can bring worried employees defences down, trust up, and empower them to buy into the organisation's change and transformation strategy.

STORYTELLING AS A TROJAN HORSE

The Trojan Horse has become a metaphor for getting behind defensive lines to create change that is impossible from the outside. These days we are not trying to get behind the walls of great cities; it's the walls employees put up that keep them disengaged.

Gallup recently conducted global research on employee engagement and found that a staggering 87% of employees worldwide are not engaged at work.

In times of change that number can be even higher because for many they don't want change, they want stability; when employees feel insecure, they become very defensive. The Trojans were the sworn enemies of the Greeks, but what about when the people with the high defences are the very people on your team and organisation? How do you get past them so you can give them the sense of security they are looking for, and also inspire a sense of bravery at the same time? How do you empower your organisation to act as a team ready to embrace the challenge of change and transformation rather than a revolt where everyone bunkers down and just looks after themselves?

The answer is to use the modern day Trojan horse: Storytelling. One of the great superpowers of storytelling is its ability to bring defensive walls down and raise the level of trust, but sometimes you need to get behind those walls first.

OVERCOMING THE STATUS QUO OF BUSINESS COMMUNICATION

We get used to transactional communication, the passing on of information because it's far more common. On a rational level, we concede communication has taken place, we intellectualise it, but we don't feel it.

Then there is transformative communication, done most effectively in narrative format, which is the passing on of purpose. This does the work needed on a rational level, but it also does the far greater work that can only happen on an emotional level. It stops the chatter in our heads; we focus, we gaze in silent fascination. We know something significant is taking place, something that had to be experienced to be truly appreciated.

Competent leaders communicate on a rational level. Great leaders communicate beyond the rational level; they communicate on an emotional level also. They want more than a transaction to take place; they want a transformation to happen.

Transformational communication is about transferring meaning, not just information. Transformational communication happens through establishing an emotional connection. The recipient needs to feel something. Without feeling, without a genuine connection, we end up with just the illusion that communication has taken place.

I believe this is what George Bernard Shaw was talking about when he famously said:

"The single biggest problem in communication is the illusion that it has taken place."

It's not enough to share information. If you want results, if you want the recipient to get the meaning behind your communication, you need to establish a connection, and everyone involved in the communication needs to be able to feel that connection.

Transactional leaders give orders; transformative leaders build connection because they know that without first establishing a connection, there can be no progress.

What creates the emotional connection?

Through *stories*.

Leaders that tell stories authentically and consistently, transform cultures. They capture both the attention and the imagination of their followers, and if anyone has a shot at capturing loyalty and commitment to a shared vision, they do.

"You can have the best technology, you can have the best business model, but if the storytelling isn't amazing, it won't matter. Nobody will watch."

- Jeff Bezos

Rational thinking is founded upon data. Emotional connection is founded upon stories. It's not one or the other. Great leaders understand the need for both. But leading with just the rational side is like showing people photos of the Grand Canyon; add the emotional side and suddenly you have pivoted and transported them *into* the Grand Canyon, an entirely different experience for everyone. From there, you can let them take their own photos.

"The story from Rapunzel to War and Peace is one of the basic tools invented by the human mind, for the purpose of gaining understanding. There have been great societies that did not use the wheel, but there have been no societies that did not tell stories."

Ursula K. Le Guin

Innovation & Employee Engagement

Everyone wanted to know how he did it. How did Jobs disrupt yet another entire industry? At the time, every conference was buzzing with the word 'disruption', and it seemed like every young entrepreneur was near obsessed with disrupting a marketplace, any marketplace. "How did he disrupt an entire industry, again?" was the conversation the movers and shakers were having amongst themselves.

When they finally got around to asking Jobs himself, his

answer was unexpected: "When we created the iTunes Music Store, we did that because we thought it would be great to be able to buy music electronically, not because we had plans to redefine the music industry."

Jobs wasn't obsessed with the concept of disrupting things; rather, his obsession was in finding solutions to problems. He was driven by an authentic passion for creating new possibilities, and that made all the difference. An authentic passion to solve difficult problems wasn't just a trait of Steve Jobs; it's common of all the great innovators throughout time. They thrive on purpose, and that's what everyone else ultimately buys into also.

Jobs also understood the importance of storytelling within his role as a leader and as an innovator. He didn't just create products; he created heroes out of his products. And along with heroes he created villains out of the status quo products and mindsets in the marketplace. He positioned Apple and its products as the hero on its own hero's journey, and for every customer who bought into Apple and their products, they too were swept up in the narrative and became heroes, too.

Jobs believed the person who had the capacity and initiative to be a storyteller in business was the most powerful of all leaders. He built his business on the foundation of storytelling, not just when he was on stage creating epic narratives for people to connect with but in the building of Apple as a whole. To Jobs, storytelling was never a gimmick or a marketing thing, but a powerful communication method; one that could not just help a business grow, but could help organisations, and even individuals, put a dint in the universe.

PURPOSE DRIVES INNOVATION

It was Spielberg's big break. He was a young filmmaker with a small budget and a great script; just enough to get his film made. He also had a big star—15 metres long. His mechanical shark was set to be the big attraction for his debut film.

But as they began production, the mechanical shark kept malfunctioning. Time and budget were tight, and the risk in stopping filming to fix the shark each time it malfunctioned was significant, for it might have resulted in them running out of cash and canning the film altogether. Steve and his team decided to pivot, adjust the script, and make the 'unseen' shark the new star, essentially shooting footage of the water instead, and adding some music to let the audience know Jaws was lurking nearby (dunt-dunt, dunt-dunt).

What looked like a colossal set back for Steven Spielberg, turned out to be an extraordinary opportunity to improve the film. What would Jaws be without the music and the tension of the unseen shark?

Spielberg knew the purpose behind his film, so when the practical way he was intending to bring that purpose to life didn't work out, he could shift to find another practical way. The shark was never the point, the story was. For organisations, if the product is the point, then once that product stops working in the marketplace, they are lost. But if they are purpose led, and the product is just an expression of their purpose, they can pivot when a product or service is no longer relevant in the marketplace and have enough clarity and direction to find a new way to serve the marketplace with their purpose.

Fixing the obvious malfunction isn't the solution, and most companies get that. Some companies are spending time and money trying to fix them, at the same time others are pivoting while they still have time and money to do so and looking for another solution, another way to innovate and win, another way to move forward without the original star product or service keeping its status. It's creating some unprecedented change in organisations. It's hard to accept a great product or service that has been profitable for many years is no longer the product or service to lead you into the future. Sometimes it takes a looming crisis to spur on an innovative new solution. Without courage, without vision, it's easy to let groupthink keep focused on fixing the malfunction and sticking to the status quo rather than innovating. In the age of massive disruption of industries, there are plenty of businesses freaking out that their big mechanical sharks are malfunctioning. The smart ones are choosing transformation instead, but with innovation comes a lot of change, and you have to bring everyone on the journey of change if you want it to be successful.

Online and offline disruption isn't going to slow down. Traditional businesses can't hide from the changing marketplace—but they can innovate. The opportunity is bleak if the focus remains on what they are losing, but it's massive if they can shift their focus on what they can gain with a new, courageous strategy. Many businesses are acutely aware of these disruptions and are in the process of making the bold changes required, but making the changes is just part of the process; communicating the change in a way that makes a genuine connection, that inspires, and that engages all the employees you need to take on the journey is critical.

If you are planning for transformation, part of that plan has to be the commitment to communicate with stories. Without buy-in, plans fail. Details don't facilitate buy-in. Head nods, sure; real connection, unlikely. The question is why risk it? Every company that wants to lead their people on a transformational journey should stack the odds of success in their favour through communicating for maximum genuine connection across their organisation. Storytelling isn't a marketing thing to tag on at the end as an afterthought; it's a strategic communication tool to help facilitate success from end to end. Plan for transformation. Communicate it with stories.

HELPING EMPLOYEES FIND THEIR CONNECTION TO INNOVATIVE TRANSFORMATION

In recent years, KPMG has drawn more on storytelling as a strategy to bring their employees together, to engage them, and get more buy-in to many transformation projects the company is implementing.

They recently created a new initiative called The Lighthouse Engagement Award. It came about as the leadership planned on transforming a key part of their business. The question they asked themselves was how they could make the changes real for employees? How could they get them to connect and embrace the changes? How could they get employees to believe the changes weren't just management playing theoretical games, but that these changes were real and beneficial for everyone? They knew from experience that employee buy-in was critical, and getting them to comply wasn't the hard part; helping them change their mindset was the challenge. If they could do that, they could dramatically increase their odds of success.

The awards program revolves around storytelling. "Employee engagement and storytelling are starting to go hand in hand," Reena explained. "Leaders are starting to understand we need to connect at the head and heart level, and more so at the heart level. Unless we connect with people at the deeper emotional level, we simply won't get the buy-in we need for our transformational plans."

The initiative works on three levels: local, regional, and global. On a local level leaders are encouraged to collect stories from their teams that exemplify their local practices, how their work impacts them as well as their clients, and how the changed processes and methodology has created new opportunities and better employee experience. The best of these stories are then shared at a regional level through event days. The presenters with the most impactful stories are then invited to share them again at a global event.

The Lighthouse Engagement Award has helped further develop a storytelling culture throughout KPMG, encouraging and empowering people to share stories about the projects they are involved in and how they have used the new tools and methodology that underpinned the company's transformation strategy. The program is set up with a large range of categories to ensure all employees have the opportunity to contribute meaningfully and reinforces that when employees choose to engage and contribute, they are heard, appreciated, and rewarded.

THE STORYTELLING STRATEGY

The power of storytelling is well documented. It is a profoundly human way of communicating. When aiming to communicate a strategy, remember that the majority don't understand the numbers, nor does everyone understand the complexity of the changing marketplace, but they all understand stories on a deep, intuitive level.

Essentially, we are all storytelling experts on a subconscious level. Think about when you watch a movie. You are automatically interpreting the film through your emotions. You are detecting if the story is authentic or fake, you connect or not with the subtext and if the characters have integrity or not; you make judgements on a range of things, but it doesn't happen rationally. Stories tap into our deeper intuitive judgment.

Our heads are more into analysis. That's why trying to lay out the facts, the numbers, the rational reasons for the change aren't going to make employees budge. Our analytical mind is used mostly to disqualify things, to defer on decisions, to void contracts, to protect its own interests. What you want to do is empower employees to use their deeper intuitive judgment faculties, where they make decisions based on purpose, not self-preservation. To do that, you need to lead discussions through a narrative structure. You need to bring people into a storytelling framework and allow the learning, the communication, and the decision to align with the strategy rather than sabotage it. This doesn't take place in the head. It will happen intuitively. It's native to us humans. Research from McKinsey and Company shows that 70% of all transformations fail. Storytelling can increase the odds. It can be a game changer.

When an organisation goes through a restructure and pivots into a new bold direction, it needs to lead thousands of individuals, too. How do you do that? How do you take hundreds or thousands of people who are resistant to change, who have a natural inclination to retreat in times of perceived danger, who are looking for anchors of safety, who are scared of losing their jobs?

If they go with the change, transformation can take place that will benefit everyone. If they don't, they will sabotage the change and force the organisation itself to retreat.

The stakes are high. Time is in short supply. Change, by its nature, is something in motion. There isn't time to stand still, yet without effective communication and collaboration with employees, the risk is the whole strategy fails.

If you want your organisation to make money, you don't necessarily need a story. A carrot and a stick will still do the trick, albeit painfully. If, however, you want your organisation and the collective employees within it to operate with purpose, storytelling is essential. When it comes to influencing the outworking of an authentic purpose, the carrot and stick aren't enough. A story that expresses the authentic purpose of the business inspires employees to work with transformational effectiveness, not just transactional effectiveness. Think big, start with a story.

CAN STORYTELLING SAVE THE DAY?

Yes, but there's a catch (and it's a good one). Facilitating communication through storytelling can be used as one of the most effective communication tools available to increase the chance of success, but it's important to recognise that storytelling on its own doesn't accomplish much.

We have all heard stories that have fallen flat, that haven't connected, that we intuitively judged to be inauthentic. This is all part of what makes storytelling a superpower. It can't be used for fakery. It only works with authenticity. So, if the organisation doesn't have a true and noble purpose; if it's just trying to hoodwink its employees into following the strategy, storytelling won't work.

But if the strategy, the change, the bold, transformative vision, is authentic, then storytelling is the greatest tool in an organisation's communication toolkit. It will create magic where every other tool just passes on information. It will reach into the deeper, intuitive space within an employees, the place where the inner hero lives, the place where they hear the call to adventure and respond.

You need your employees to find their courage, to understand that a transformation of the organisation is an opportunity for personal transformation, also. That a change to succeed in the future marketplace for the organisation ensures a successful future for the employees.

When a company is in the midst of change and transformation, it inevitably feels the pressure of resistance from thousands of nervous employees. When this happens, the solution isn't to figure it out with your head; you have to go deeper. The winning solution is to think about how all employees are human, and while technology evolves fast, the essential human functions don't; we all identify with stories; that's how we decide who to trust, who's telling the truth, and who is worth following. Storytelling is how people connect, engage, and feel the prompting to make decisions.

Stories help people renew their motivation, embrace their value, and boost their courage. Stories capture focus, create trust, and empower agreement. Stories move people to take action, make decisions, and move forward. Storytelling isn't a novelty; it's a change agent. Want change? Want progress? Communicate it with stories.

"Storytelling is the oldest form of education."

Terry Tempest Williams

AUTHENTICITY
& COURAGE

One day a young man was walking down a busy side street in the middle of town when he noticed a small new shop. It was unusual because it was the only shop with no customers inside. To either side, people were busy purchasing shirts and watches, and the latest gizmos. The empty shop was selling none of these modern items; instead, it was selling values.

The young man wandered inside and discovered to his

amazement that indeed the shop was selling values. He approached the counter, asking, "Can I purchase any value I wish?"

The shopkeeper nodded, "Of course. Which one would you like, sir?"

The young man fidgeted on the spot, then spoke up, stating, "Well, lately I've been thinking a lot about authenticity. I would like to be authentic in my job, but I feel I often end up playing the corporate game and wearing a kind of mask instead. I have tried to be authentic myself, but haven't succeeded." He looked up and smiled, "But if I can simply purchase it, that would be great!"

The shopkeeper nodded, "Of course, sir. You can certainly purchase it today."

"How much does it cost?" the man asked, reaching for his wallet.

"It depends on how much you want," the shopkeeper replied.

"I want it all!" the man said enthusiastically.

"No problem, sir."

"Yes, yes, no problem," the young man repeated. "Tell me, what is the price?"

The shopkeeper replied, "For one hundred percent authenticity, the price you need to pay is one hundred percent courage."

The young man paused, thought for a moment, then asked, "Can I pay on credit?"

The shopkeeper shook his head, "Sorry sir, this kind of payment is required up front."

THE PRICE OF AUTHENTICITY IN WORK AND LIFE

Rajendra Agrawal is the former General Manager of the State Bank of India and now spends his time lecturing at one of India's top management schools on ethics. A topic that is close to his heart is authenticity in the workplace. When I asked him why he thought it was hard for leaders to be authentic in the workplace, instead of giving me a data-driven answer, he told me a version of the above story. In doing so, he brought home his point with great clarity.

"Living authentically is about living courageously; to live that way, you have to accept a level of risk as part of the process. If there were nothing risky about it, it wouldn't be considered courageous."

Rajendra gave me a sense of calmness when I talked with him. He was more interested in listening to my thoughts, to learn himself, than to talk. I thought that was admirable, not because he wanted to listen to me, but because he wanted to listen in general; I believe being willing to listen deeply is a universal sign of wisdom.

But he also shared his thoughts with me freely, and one of the things he said stuck with me. We were talking about how we have created this big divider between work and life, and we try to live authentically in life, but readily accept a compromise at work. This can be agreed upon on a conscious level, but on a deeper human level, the conflict can create internal tension and disruption. When we don't act courageously to be authentic in the workplace, we lose a sense of our true self in our personal lives also.

What is the result of this inner conflict? Rajendra thinks it is the feeling of emptiness and unhappiness.

"Authenticity is the only remedy for misery," Rajendra said. "You can't compartmentalise your life. It is another fallacy. The idea that in my personal life I can be deeply faithful to my true self, but when I go into business, because it is a jungle, I play games. It just doesn't work. To be fulfilled—to be happy—you need to aim for 100% authenticity."

But many of Rajendra's students struggle with authenticity. Like most, they want to be authentic, but just don't see how they can truly do it without risking their ability to climb the corporate ladder, or even ensure they keep their job. It's a challenge not just for the students, but for all of us. It's risky, but the risk isn't really about the risk of missing a promotion as much as it is about the risk of being honest with ourselves. That, in many cases, is what we are most concerned about because authenticity isn't about character, or ethics, or nobility; it's not about being good or bad—it's about being true to self. Maybe the true remedy for unhappiness in the workplace is through creating more opportunity for employees to find their courage to be more authentic?

Perhaps true happiness is found in calming the conflict within? To remove that conflict, we all need to visit that metaphorical little shop down the side street of town, and pay for our authenticity upfront, and in full.

"Tell me, what is the price?"

The shopkeeper replied, "For 100% authenticity, the price you need to pay is 100% courage."

STORYTELLING TAKES AUTHENTICITY AND REQUIRES COURAGE

Sure, storytelling is a great way to market your wares; it's a great sales strategy. But it's like yoga; it doesn't just fix one thing, it fixes almost everything. I encourage you to think of storytelling not as a marketing thing but a human thing; as long as you are working with humans, bringing storytelling more to the centre of your communication strategy is a winning move.

One of the hidden benefits of storytelling is the key elements required. I'm not talking about the elements of the story itself, but of the individual telling the story.

Storytelling requires courage, and when employees start acting with more courage, teams start working better together, ideas get expressed and actioned, and business grows.

The reason storytelling requires courage is that you *feel* when you tell a story. It's very different than when you pass on data. When you pass on data, you don't feel if people are connecting or disconnecting. It's not an emotional experience. It's mechanical. But storytelling is human, and that means if a story bombs, you *feel* it—and so do the people listening—and it's uncomfortable. The risk is people retreat to data-talk, not because it's more effective, but because it's less risky. The paradox is it is very risky, but the risk then sits with the organisation, because if staff and leaders are not communicating effectively, business is sabotaged.

Creating a storytelling culture where leaders lead by example, where they face the risk of feeling uncomfortable, and in doing so also exhibit vulnerability, is transformational. Trust begets trust. If leaders can tell stories where some work like magic and some go pear-shaped, but through it all the culture encourages and affirms storytelling as an important communication tool, then team members can reciprocate; they can also find their courage and tell their stories, they can risk the feeling of a story falling short when they know that is part of the process, that others do it, and together a strong storytelling culture can be built.

This process also leads to building a more authentic communication culture, because the major reason stories bomb is not that the story is bad, but that it is missing some of the key ingredients. These elements of the human condition are very difficult to measure and impossible to demand, but through a storytelling strategy, where storytelling becomes part of the organisation's culture, it can be developed, it can be set up as a teachable process, and it can give your organisation the edge in our ever-changing world.

HOW IMPORTANT IS COURAGE IN TODAY'S WORKPLACE?

If you want a workplace with genuine connections, with integrity toward its stated values and where compromise doesn't drown out authenticity, it's critical. Without it, employees can end up accepting the long-held notion that compromise is part of business, and it's better to remain silent and let things slide.

Clinging to the status quo as a source of comfort may have worked in yesteryear, but the strategy of sticking to the status quo is no longer relevant. In today's disrupted marketplace, the status quo is not a driver of commercial viability. 'This is the way we've always done it,' is an outdated mindset, and moving to being obsolete at an increasing pace.

Change requires courage. The world is changing at a rapid rate (and it will never be this slow to change again. Think about that!). We are entering a world and a marketplace where companies who empower employees to change and innovate the business will win, and those who maintain a workforce who cling to the status quo of yesterday will struggle.

This is nothing new. We all know that every industry in the marketplace is being disrupted and this will only continue to happen. But I wonder how many leaders have correlated the level of courage in their teams with the level of successful innovation and change? This isn't just about having 'light bulb' moments and pulling an entirely new product line into the business. It's about culture as much as anything. There is a deeply human element to it.

I think the winning edge between companies these days is around company culture and who remains true to their stated beliefs. The most talented, in-demand employees are asking questions such as: Which company has a genuine culture? What company really lives and breathes its values? What company demonstrates its vision in a diverse and tangible way? Which company can I trust based on watching how their current employees speak and act online? Which company has the most compelling purpose, backed up by proof it is living that purpose?

A living and active culture, that is real and true to its stated core values, has never been more important; it's a key driver for recruiting and retaining talent, and, through synergy and productivity, facilitates greater commercial success; however, it's not just in the hands of an organisation to create a great company culture, individual employees also need to grow personally, and develop a greater sense of self-awareness. Without self-awareness, it's hard for someone to know what they truly stand for and believe in, and if they don't have clarity about these things, then they won't have the courage to stand up in defence of them.

WHAT MADE GE LIVE A SUCCESS?

When Joanne received the nod from the GE leadership on creating her vision of a storytelling event, she began connecting with employees from all different areas of the business. She wasn't looking for expert presenters; rather, she was looking for authentic stories. Where were they, what were they, and how can they amplify them so others can be inspired by them? Her team found ten employees with a story that would have universal appeal to all employees and each one was coached in storytelling over the course of four months. When the event finally came around, 300 employees were in the auditorium, including the CEO and other senior leaders. Backstage, one of the last speakers for the day stood waiting.

Jenny wasn't a public speaker. She was an ordinary employee. Saying she was nervous was an understatement. She was terrified. Jenny was one of ten employees invited to share their story and Joanne had personally coached her over the past few months on storytelling to get her ready for her ten-minute talk. They both felt she had a great, authentic story to share—but now it was not just an idea, it was happening.

The crowd clapped as Jenny took her place on stage and began her talk, but almost immediately she fell silent having lost her way. She stood frozen for a full thirty seconds.

Jenny looked down to the front row. Joanne was there, motioning with encouragement for her to continue. She tried starting her story again only to freeze again.

She stood again for another 30 seconds in silence, her eyes

locked on Joanne.

"Hang in there," Joanne thought. This was the moment Jenny could run. She could leave the stage and hide. She could have given up and said, 'I'm not good at this.' But she also had the choice to find her courage and continue.

The entire room waited in nervous anticipation.

Jenny eyed backstage, but instead of giving up she found her courage and her story once again; for the next eight minutes she found her flow and shared her story brilliantly. Her talk ended with a standing ovation.

GE Live did more than just showcase the great work GE was doing around the country; it gave employees the opportunity to engage peer-to-peer, to be authentic and vulnerable; to be real and to be brave. That kind of connection wouldn't happen with a slick, faultless multimedia presentation; it couldn't happen with an information dump—but it did happen when an everyday employee was courageous enough to share her authentic story, to overcome her nerves and hurdles, and to risk vulnerability in the process of building a connection.

Jenny was also the people's choice as the best speaker of the event. Despite her nerves. Despite freezing on stage twice, something very powerful happened—the audience connected with her; they witnessed her being brave and sharing from her heart. She wasn't technically faultless, but her message was incredibly memorable, and it had a lasting impact on the audience. It was risky. It could have failed. But we must remember it's far riskier to stick to the status quo, to play it safe, and to ignore we are living in a world of massive disruption and what every business needs is not 'safe', it needs genuine passion and connection, it needs a culture that will be agile and supportive rather than siloed and defensive. GE Live didn't just give people an opportunity to share a story, on a deeper level it created the opportunity for people to be brave.

WHY AUTHENTICITY MATTERS AT WORK

Jacqui McNamara is the head of Security at Telstra and a passionate advocate for authenticity in the workplace. She agrees with Rajendra's insights that authenticity is tied to courage, and believes this is what ultimately creates a more genuine company culture that lives their shared values.

"I think the real value of authenticity is how it creates courage to ask the hard question, rather than just letting things slide. That's why it's so important to have a clear understanding of who you are. It helps you get clear on your values and allows you to act with more consistent integrity. Without self-awareness, you can't understand why X doesn't sit right with you, or Y doesn't sit right with you."

Courage in the workplace requires clarity on one's guiding principles. If you don't know your true north, it's hard to know if things are aligned with your own values. Self-awareness helps you grow and develop personally, and through finding your own set of values, it allows you to engage authentically with the company's values when they are in alignment.

Jacqui also believes self-awareness creates more acceptance in the workplace, for self and for others, and can play a pivotal role in actual business deliverables being a success rather than a failure. That fine line comes down to how individuals use their energy, either to build the business or to maintain their corporate image.

"You have to have a good understanding of who you are in order to be authentic. If you are scared to simply be yourself in the workplace, a lot of energy is needed to be someone you're not. When that happens with enough people, it makes it difficult to create a culture where people feel safe to be themselves."

STORYTELLING TO BUILD EMOTIONAL INTELLIGENCE

This is where the power of storytelling in the workforce lies.

It can cause some individuals to courageously use their energy to propel the purpose of the business forward; through a storytelling culture, creating the environment of trust and openness is possible, and it can allow the majority of employees to connect, align, and engage with one another and the purpose of the organisation.

Building teams that grow in their emotional intelligence, in their self-awareness, and in their desire to live out their personal and professional lives with authenticity may not seem like a major factor in an organisation's success, but they may just deliver the critical few inches needed to win the game.

This is what makes storytelling so powerful in the workplace. It's not storytelling itself, but the things it empowers. We all know that emotional intelligence is critical, but it's also really hard to teach. Indeed, most employees who need it the most would be most resistant to any discussion let alone training on building their emotional intelligence capabilities. But what about learning how to be better storytellers? This has far less resistance while also being more intriguing and interesting to employees. Through developing employees storytelling capabilities, a natural knock-on effect is the building of their emotional intelligence.

You don't feel data, but you always feel stories. Even when you don't feel the connection, you still feel the disconnection. That's because our emotions are hardwired to give and react to prompts in stories. By investing time, focus, and resources into building an authentic storytelling culture you also are investing in building a higher level of emotional intelligence in your teams, because you can't tell effective stories without exploring your own authenticity, becoming open to vulnerability and choosing to be more self-aware.

Storytelling can drive all the business-driven outcomes; more engagement, more productivity, more profits; but more important than this is how storytelling naturally leads employees to tap into their humanity rather than hide behind the corporate veil; in a world where machine learning and artificial intelligence will be infinitely better at crunching the numbers and analysing data, it is our humanity that will ultimately be our point of difference in the marketplace of the future. By creating and developing a storytelling culture and elevating storytelling in all your communication strategies you will certainly get better business results, but you will get more than that in the deal; you'll also get employees turning up willing to contribute to the organisation with their single greatest asset: *their humanity.*

"Storytelling is the essential human activity. The harder the situation, the more essential it is."

Tim O'Brien

IMPLEMENTING THE STORYTELLING SUPERPOWER

How did neuroscientist turned storytelling-advocate Paul Zak convince the military it was a good idea to train their soldiers in the craft of storytelling?

The short answer is he didn't. The connection came about through a new recruit in their management team who already believed in the value and ability of storytelling to build trust and reduce conflict. During one of their meetings, while the others leaders at the table were talking about traditional military strategies for reducing risk to their soldiers and civilians in emotionally charged environments, the new guy made a left-field suggestion: the military should be open to exploring implementing a storytelling strategy.

You can imagine the initial resistance. After all, they weren't Hollywood. They weren't in the entertainment business. What they were dealing with was life and death. However, to their credit they remained open to the suggestion, and once they saw the research that outlined the science behind storytelling and the specific pathway it could provide to achieving the outcomes they desired, they agreed to test the waters.

What started as a small project to train a select few to review and evaluate the outcomes, ended up becoming a large-scale project that spanned several years, training up an extensive range of soldiers in the craft of storytelling.

Like the military, the vast majority of businesses aren't in the entertainment business; they're not selling stories like Hollywood does, yet storytelling can and should still play a pivotal role in any business strategy. The reason is simple: We are all human. Sure, we can function in business without stories, but it's hard to genuinely connect without them. The built-in ability of stories to reduce conflict, establish trust, create an environment of true collaboration shouldn't be ignored; alternatively, they should be leveraged to produce even greater business outcomes.

Employees are first and foremost humans. The day and age where humans felt like a mechanical cog in the wheel belongs in the past. With a future workplace and employee mindset already experiencing an enormous shift away from the past, businesses need to find new and effective ways of not just engaging their staff, but also inspiring them with purpose. The consumers of tomorrow's world are looking to organisations that have a genuine purpose that its own employees have internalised and embrace in their everyday work. Storytelling is the most effective communication tool to not only reach consumers but also to reach their own employees. Storytelling in business isn't a marketing thing. It's a human thing. It belongs in every department; it can make possible what no other form of communication can accomplish. It's been at the very apex of our existence since the dawn of civilisation. It's what taps into our deepest emotions and desires; it's what makes us feel alive. It's what makes us find our courage to take action.

There are many ways to implement storytelling into a business, but the starting point is to first recognise its value and see it as a potential superpower to be activated in your organisation. From there, you can start small or large, but you have to start; you have to accept the challenge and the upside of implementing stories into your everyday workflow, into your business planning, and ultimately into your overall communication strategy.

Storytelling works at work.

Trust me, I'm human.

About The Author

Mick is a passionate communicator and storyteller. He is an accomplished author, mentor, professional trainer and keynote speaker. He believes storytelling is both the most effective and the most engaging way to lead people through change and onwards to personal and professional transformation. He also moonlights as a husband and father of two wild and wonderful kids.

Connect with Mick at: **www.mickmooney.com**

WORK WITH MICK

If you would like Mick to speak at your next event or would like to learn more about his training & mentoring programs, you can connect with him at his website: mickmooney.com

Other ways to connect:
email: mick@mickmoney.com
linkedin.com/in/mickmooney
twitter.com/mick_mooney
facebook.com/mickmooney.author

MENTIONS

Gary Vaynerchuk is a Belarusian American entrepreneur, author, speaker and internet personality and founder of VaynerMedia | garyvaynerchuk.com

Joanne Woo is the VP of Communications for Australia and New Zealand at GE. She's also the curator for TEDx Melbourne. | Ge.com | tedxmelbourne.com

Forbes: https://www.forbes.com/sites/billeehoward/2016/04/04/storytelling-the-new-strategic-imperative-of-business/#4d52fd9b4d79

Swampy Marsh is the Senior Director of Client Advocacy at Dimension Data | dimensiondata.com

The prison in India is called Sanganer Camp. I initially heard about this in Paul Zak's book Trust Factor

Reena Malik is the ASPAC Regional Director - Head of People Development at KPMG | http://kpmg.com

Paul Zak is the founding director of the Center for Neuroeconomics | www.pauljzak.com

Why Storytelling Works at Work

Seth Godin is an American bestselling author and former dot com business executive | sethgodin.com

Suits is an American legal drama television series created and written by Aaron Korsh. The series premiered on June 23, 2011, on the cable network USA, and is produced by Universal Cable. Suits is set at a fictional law firm in New York City. | en.wikipedia.org/wiki/Suits_(U.S._TV_series)

Daniel Pink is a New York Times and Wall Street Journal bestselling author | danpink.com

Antonio Damasio is a Portuguese-American neuroscientist. He is currently the David Dornsife Professor of Neuroscience, Psychology and Philosophy at the University of Southern California and an adjunct professor at the Salk Institute. | antoniodamasio.com

Microsoft study on attention spans | scribd.com/document/265348695/Microsoft-Attention-Spans-Research-Report

Grant Cardone is a New York Times bestselling author, international speaker, business innovator, social media personality and top sales trainer in the world | grantcardone.com

TED Talks are influential videos from expert speakers on education, business, science, tech and creativity, with subtitles in 100+ languages. Ideas free to stream and download. | ted.com

RSL stands for Returned and Services League. It is an Australian support organisation for men and women who have served or are serving in the Defence Force but is open to the whole community for drinking, dining and entertainment. | rslnational.org

Walker research on Customer Experience 2020 |
https://www.walkerinfo.com/knowledge-center/webcasts/customers-2020

Steve Jobs was an American entrepreneur, business magnate, inventor, and industrial designer. He was the chairman, chief executive officer (CEO), and a co-founder of Apple Inc | apple.com

Sir Richard Branson is an English business magnate, investor and philanthropist. He founded the Virgin Group, which controls more than 400 companies. | virgin.com

Roger Carl Schank (born 1946) is an American artificial intelligence theorist, cognitive psychologist, learning scientist, educational reformer, and entrepreneur | rogerschank.com

The Trojan Horse is a tale from the Trojan War about the subterfuge that the Greeks used to enter the independent city of Troy and win the war. In the canonical version, after a fruitless 10-year siege, the Greeks constructed a huge wooden horse, and hid a select force of men inside.

Uri Hasson is a Professor in the Psychology Department and the Neuroscience Institute at Princeton University | hassonlab.com

Gallup employee engagement results |
http://www.gallup.com/services/190118/engagedworkplace.aspx

George Bernard Shaw was an Irish playwright, critic, polemicist, and political activist |

Jeffrey Bezos is an American technology and retail entrepreneur, investor, electrical engineer, computer scientist, and philanthropist, best known as the founder, chairman, and chief executive officer of Amazon | amazon.com

Ursula Kroeber Le Guin was an American novelist. She worked mainly in the genres of fantasy and science fiction

McKinsey & Company is the trusted advisor and counselor to many of the world's most influential businesses and institutions | https://www.mckinsey.com/industries/retail/our-insights/the-how-of-transformation

Terry Tempest Williams, is an American author, conservationist, and activist | coyoteclan.com

Rajendra Agrawal is an Indian businessman and teacher

Jacqui McNamara is the head of Security at Telstra | telstra.com

Tim O'Brien is an American novelist |

BONUS SECTION

HOW TO USE STORIES TO CREATE ENGAGING CONTENT

At the time of publishing this book I did a keynote on Storytelling For Business for the Australian Institute of Training and Development. The event was hosted at Linked HQ in Sydney, and our Linkedin host for the event was Jorn Are Lundi, Learning and Development Strategist at Linkedin Australia.

Both Rebecca from AITD and Jorn from Linkedin were awesome hosts and it was a great evening. The next day, Jorn sent me an email:

> *Thank you so much for presenting yesterday. It was really great and I got some good takeaways from you. I'll try to implement this and make a note of my observations.*

Two weeks later I got another email, this time it read:

> *Good news! The leadership has been so impressed with my storytelling that we are now running a program to upskill all managers.*

Like anyone seeking to add value and make a difference in their work, I was excited to hear how Jorn had applied what he learned, and consequently the knock-on effect it started in his organisation.

Fast forward a few weeks and Jorn and I are enjoying a hot drink and discussing a variety of innovative learning and development initiatives and how they can be used to empower organisations through periods of change and transformation, and how storytelling can be used to help support those outcomes.

Thought leadership as a learning and development tool

We got onto the topic of thought leadership to empower learning and development through written content, such as articles on Linkedin. I shared a simple framework with Jorn I use when crafting Linkedin articles (though it can be used to create any business content). I wanted to share this method with you, as you also might find it a helpful framework when seeking to create content that is engaging and valuable for your target reader.

The SIC Method for crafting engaging content

This simple framework can help you create compelling content that resonates with your target audience. You need to ensure you use the following three elements: SIC stands for _Stories, Insight,_ and _Context._ Here's how you can apply it:

Stories

It's a good habit to start every article with a story. The reason is simple: it buys you time with your reader. As humans, we understand stories. We know they unfold. We accept we won't understand them from the first line, that we need to read or listen further to get the payoff. This is very different to mere information. When it comes to information, we want to understand it immediately or we lose interest. Most of the time we are bored before we even finish the first sentence of information—but this doesn't happen with stories.

By starting with a story you are drawing your reader in; they are willing to invest more time to read, and the more time they invest the more determined they will be to get an ROI on that investment; that encourages them to keep reading—but you have to hold up your end of the deal. There needs to be an ROI, a payoff for reading, and that's where the next element comes into play.

Insight

Stories are like chimes. When you hit a chime, it resonates for a period of time. The same is true for stories. When you tell them, afterwards the interest of the reader remains, the story is still resonating, and that is the chance to share your insights. To be able to do this, you have to be able to springboard off the story. In other words, the story has to have the same theme as the insights you want to share. Think of the story as the gift wrapping, and the insights the gift. This is your chance to share your insights with the reader, and the more you can bring your own thoughts and ideas into this section, the better, because readers connect with personality, with authenticity, and with vulnerability. By sharing your own thoughts within your insights, rather than just curating others thoughts, you continue to keep the reader interested enough for the final element.

Context

This is where you turn your focus to the reader directly. Do you have enough clarity on what you are sharing through your stories and insights to conclude with some takeaways for the target reader? If you can, you've hit gold. Thinking of how the stories and insights might affect the reader in context to their own life, and some questions for them to ask themselves, or some advice on how to put the contents of your article into practice is where you deliver on the ROI for their time.

Keep It Simple

The SIC method isn't bulletproof, it's not a hard and fast rule, and of course there are other effective ways to write compelling articles—but it can be a helpful guide when seeking to craft an engaging article within a limited timeframe. It can also help you get clarity upfront, to figure out the three elements and how they hang together, and have more confidence that what you share will be of value to readers.

Creating an article that unpacks your thought leadership doesn't have to take hours, and nor should it; but it is meant to add value to your target audience, create a connection with them, and help them learn something. If you want to lead and develop business through being of service, adding value, and solving problems, then being a content creator should be high on your priority list.

You can add a lot of value to in the marketplace by sharing your thoughts on your area of interest and expertise. To get started, keep it simple: Start with a *story*, roll into your *insights*, and close with *context*—then get back to business.

Repeat regularly, and everyone wins.

On the following pages I have added a few article that follow this method as examples of how this method can be applied.

Trust Me, I'm Human

EXAMPLE ONE

THE POWER OF MENTORS—AND WHY YOU NEED TO FIND ONE IF ONE HASN'T FOUND YOU YET

A little girl was sitting in a doctor's office staring at the floor while her mother spoke with the doctor. The mother was desperate. She wanted some medication to 'fix' her troubled child. She had been officially warned by the School Headmaster to get her daughter professional help, or she would have to be removed from the school.

According to her teachers, the little girl was irritated, disruptive, and had a learning disorder. Before they left the room, the doctor advised the little girl he would step outside the room for a few minutes with her mother, and put on some music to keep her entertained while she waited.

Once alone, the mother began explaining again what was wrong with her daughter, and asking what he could do to fix her—but the doctor did not answer her. He was captivated by the little girl inside, who had immediately gotten up, jumped on his desk and leapt off all in rhythm with the music. She danced all around the room, having the most fabulous time. Watching the little girl through the door glass, a heart-warming smile emerged on his face. He turned to the mother and said, "There's nothing wrong with your daughter, she's just in the wrong room. She's a dancer. Put her in dance school."

A few days later the mother did put her in dance school, and the little girl was overjoyed; for the first time, she felt she was in a room where the other kids were just like her. Finally, she was in the right room. That little girl was Gillian Lynne, the now legendary dancer who choreographed "Cats," and "Phantom Of The Opera," and considered to be Broadway royalty.

The most watched TED talk of all time

This story was made famous by Sir Ken Robinson, who shared it in his TED talk, which is also the most watched TED talk of all time. What made his talk resonate so deeply with so many people? It was on education, but there are many educational TED talks. I don't think it was the theme that was so appealing, but the power of his stories, most significantly this one. Why this one?

Because we've all felt at one point (perhaps we still feel it?) in our lives that something is wrong, that we are in the wrong room. But I don't believe that is why the story appeals to us. It's because at a very deep, emotional level, we long for someone like the doctor to come into our lives, someone who can see what others can't, our inner genius, and also had the foresight to explain we are in the wrong room and what the right room is. For most of us, perhaps we are still hoping to meet such a person, and to find that right room?

We are all on a Hero's Journey

Joseph Campbell was a researcher on mythology and storytelling. After studying thousands of stories and myths from a range of different sources, ages, cultures and religions, he noticed a common pattern. He called it the Hero with a thousand faces. Essentially, Campbell believed that almost every epic story that had garnered mass and lasting appeal, had at its core the same story structure: the story of the hero on a life-changing journey who meets a range of characters that help & hinder him, and who must face and overcome many obstacles and setbacks along their way to eventual victory.

Mentors don't make you win, but it's hard to win without them

Who would Neo have become without meeting Morpheus? Who would Luke Skywalker become without Yoda? What about Frodo without meeting Gandalf? In the Hero's Journey, a defining experience is when they meet the Sage, the mentor figure that knows what they don't know, who can see what they can't see, and knows how to get to their great victory when they have no idea what victory even looks like. Don't be mistaken, the hero still needs to do the work, risk it all on an epic quest, but without the mentor they would likely not even start; doubt would take them out.

What would have become of Gillian Lynne if she had not crossed paths with that doctor? In an interview I recently heard, she attributes all of her career and success to that doctor. It's not that the doctor did the work. He didn't master the craft of dance. He didn't devote his life to being a great dancer. She did it all—but he still played a critical role. He was the pivotal moment in her journey that directed her to eventual victory.

Your own epic journey awaits

How about you? I want to encourage you to keep your eyes open for a great, authentic, and powerful mentor. For the lucky few, mentors find them; for the rest of us we have to find them. In a business world, that means you're going to have to pay for a good mentor. Don't let that hinder you because a great mentor will almost certainly cause your financial income to increase, not to mention your level of confidence and sense of satisfaction in the progress you make in a professional and personal level.

There's no doubt you're a hero. I mean that honestly. I know, because we are all heroes, it's just that most of us haven't yet truly embraced our status as a hero, we haven't truly committed to the epic journey required for victory—but we all can, and we all should.

I love the sage advice from Hellen Keller:

> *"Life is either a daring adventure or nothing. Security does not exist in nature, nor do the children of men as a whole experience it. Avoiding danger is no safer in the long run than exposure."*

It's time to embrace your inner hero. The journey awaits. If you feel you are in the wrong room, take the time to find a mentor who can help you understand what the right room for you is, and how you can get into it.

In short, choose to be epic, but don't go it alone. Get some guidance; and, if possible, a little magic from a Mentor before you truly launch into your daring adventure. Victory awaits!

EXAMPLE TWO

THE MAKING OF A WINNER'S MINDSET

"Who's the greatest now?"

It was the first time Muhammad Ali had lost a fight. Technically, he had lost once before to Joe Frazer, but that was controversial, and Ali didn't feel he lost that one. It was a technicality. But this time around, he knew. A broken jaw has a way of making a fighter feel a loss.

An uppercut in one of the opening rounds broke his jaw, but he didn't stop him. He went through the rest of the fight, round after round, protecting his face and trying to knock out the local fighter, Ken Norton. It was the only way to win the fight.

He couldn't get close enough without opening himself up. If Norton hit his jaw again, it would be life-threatening. In the end, Norton's hand was raised. Ali lost on points.

The crowd erupted and started rushing to the ring. For years many in his nation despised Ali. They hated him not just because he was a black man, but because he was a black man who dared to claim that he was the greatest. Greater than who? Everyone? Greater then *they* were? It got under their skin. In the minds of those who hated him, Ali losing to their local fighter was final proof they needed to tell him he was wrong. They went wild at the chance to let him know it.

Ali was escorted from the ring by a barrage of security guards. The crowd was screaming insults and threats. When they got Ali to his change room, while they were searching for a doctor, someone managed to push through the door just long enough to cry out, *"Who's the greatest now?"*

Who's the greatest now?

It's amazing how far apart these two people were in their mindset. One, a spectator, who waited for the opportunity to tear Ali down and to *sow doubt*; the other, a champion who worked every day for the chance to live his dream, and who *sowed belief* every day to fuel that vision.

People who heard Ali all the years prior making that claim, *I am the greatest*, thought he was boasting. They thought he was proud. They thought he was narcissistic. But it wasn't about trying to get others to believe him. Ali only wanted one person to believe it, himself; because he was the only one who could do the work to make it a reality. What he was doing was selling himself on a vision that would motivate to train harder than anyone else.

Ali made the statement, *"I am the greatest,"* to remind himself of what he was attempting to achieve. They weren't words for everyone else, but saying them loud and proud was a way to keep himself accountable. It was a way to reinforce his beliefs. They were words to himself to remind himself that he had no right to lower his ambition, no reason to be satisfied with being good, or even great; no, he had to train the way the greatest would train. He had to work harder than the greats because there could be only one greatest. He wanted to be the best he could be, and that meant his standard had to be as high as possible. Most aimed to be great. Ali aimed higher—to be the greatest.

I got me thinking about how we feel about our own lives and our ambitions.

Think about it: What do you want to be the greatest at? Not just good, not just great, but the greatest?

I tried this on myself, and I felt a tangible level of discomfort. On the surface, I think I worried about how others would perceive such an ambition. But that's not the real issue. In fact, I think that's a convenient cop out. The reason this kind of questioning is uncomfortable, I've come to conclude, is because it is connected *focus* and *effort*.

To be average, you just have to have an average amount of focus and put in an average amount of effort. But to be the greatest requires the greatest level of focus and effort. Those who are spectating think being the greatest is about the spotlight and the glory, but those who are working to be the greatest know it's about the *focus* and *effort* to get there. The mindsets are worlds apart.

Spectators and champions

It's so easy to be a spectator. It's easy to sit in the grandstand of life and watch those who dare to be great, even the greatest, and wait for a moment to pull them down. But it's a shallow life. Its highlights are dependent on the setbacks of others. Its own boast is in the pleasure of watching others fall short.

"Who's the greatest now?" The spectator said with pride. He wasn't alone in trying to pull Ali down, seeing it as the moment to make him stop with his crazy ambitions and statements of greatness. For months after his loss in the boxing ring, hate mail was sent to Ali. Messages of doubt and disgrace. One of those letters was a blank page with just two lines written in the middle. It said:

> *"The butterfly has lost its wings. The bee has lost its sting."*

Ali took that message and tapped it next to his punching bag. He was grateful for it. The writer intended it to dampen his ambition, but he used it instead as fuel. He looked at it every day as he trained for a rematch against Norton. Those words were meant to chip away at Ali's confidence and fill him with doubt, but he used them to remember who he was—*I am the greatest*—and if he had lost his wings, he had to train harder than anyone else to get them back. If he had lost his sting, he had to fight harder than anyone to get it back. That's just what he did.

He went on to beat Norton in the rematch and beat him again after that. He also went on to beat George Foreman. Eventually, he went on to be remembered not as a good fighter, or a great fighter, but as the greatest.

"Who's the greatest now?" 45 years after that spectator asked that question, the answer remains the same: Ali is.

EXAMPLE THREE

THE POWER TO CHANGE THE WORLD STARTS WITH THE STORIES WE TELL OURSELVES

Tony was just eleven years old when a strange man holding some grocery bags filled with enough food for a big Thanksgiving dinner knocked on his door. His father answered. The stranger explained he wanted of give them a turkey and some food for Thanksgiving. He didn't know them, but he knew they were on hard times (in desperation, sometimes his sister would knock on neighbours doors asking for food). Tony's father grunted, and said, "We're not a charity case!" He tried to slam the door shut, but the stranger stopped it with his foot. He leaned closer to the door, looked down at Tony who was watching in the background, then back to the father and said, "Think of your kids. Don't let your ego stop them from eating tonight."

His father reluctantly took the food and slammed the door. It was Thanksgiving, but the stranger got no thanks from his father.

The story his father made out of that moment was people thought he was a charity case, and he felt humiliated. The story that eleven-year-old Tony made out of that moment was that strangers care about him, and if strangers care about him, then he should care about strangers.

When Tony started working a few years later, that story started defining his actions; he took it upon himself to do what that stranger had done, and feed a less fortunate family for Thanksgiving, then two, then four. As his business did better, he kept multiplying the strangers he would care for. This continued for years and decades.

"Last year I fed 102 million people, which was really an outgrowth of someone feeding me when I was 11 years old when there was no money and no food." - Tony Robins

That young boy grew up to be Tony Robbins, who has now feed over 350 million disadvantaged families and intends to feed one-billion families within the next seven years. All of this was a result of two things.

1. The actions of a stranger who was moved by his heart to help.

2. The story Tony made out of that moment.

Tony's father created a completely different, negative story, and that story did not serve him or anyone else. Tony, in contrast, created a positive story and it not only served him, leading him to become the greatest life & performance coach in history, empowering millions of people through his businesses, and soon to be billions of people through his acts of charity and love for humanity . . . even if they are strangers to him.

Create better stories out of your experiences

Life is full of experiences, some great, some challenging, some light and some dark; but we still have ultimate control to define the narrative of those moments and they transfer into our memories. Tony could have also followed his father's interpretation and created the story, "My family and I are a charity case." Instead, he created the story, "Strangers care about me, and I, therefore, should care about strangers."

Create the stories that serve your desired future

What kind of life do you want to live? What kind of legacy do you want to leave behind you? Make sure you form your internal narratives in a way that supports those outcomes. If you notice the stories you tell yourself are negative, weed them out and replace them with better stories—because it is the stories we tell ourselves that ultimately create the people we become.

"Strangers care, therefore I should care about strangers." What a story that is! What is the ROI on that story? It wasn't just life-changing for Tony, but it has allowed him to truly put a dint in the universe. His influence and impact on our generation are impossible to measure.

The great life-lesson we can all learn, and should all apply

You can control the internal narrative. That's one of the greatest lessons any of us will ever learn. You are the storyteller of your own life. Don't waste the opportunity; be brave, and write an epic tale on the pages of your own heart and mind that will do more than just impact the success of your own life, but impact the well-being of an untold number of other people as well.

Trust Me, I'm Human

TRUST ME, I'M HUMAN
WHY STORYTELLING WORKS AT WORK

BY MICK MOONEY

Thanks for reading!

If you enjoyed this book, feel free to reach out to me with feedback or questions. I'd love to stay connected.

Blue skies,

Mick Mooney

mick@mickmooney.com | https://www.mickmooney.com

NOTES

NOTES

NOTES

NOTES

NOTES

NOTES

NOTES

NOTES

Trust Me, I'm Human

Why Storytelling Works at Work

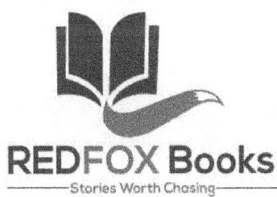

Trust Me, I'm Human

www.ingramcontent.com/pod-product-compliance
Lightning Source LLC
Chambersburg PA
CBHW031958190326
41520CB00007B/291